IMPERIAL TOMBS
OF CHINA

Imperial Tombs of China

Essays by

Lei Congyun

Senior Research Fellow
China Cultural Relics Promotion Center, Beijing

Yang Yang

Associate Senior Research Fellow
China Cultural Relics Promotion Center, Beijing

Zhao Gushan

Research Fellow
China Cultural Relics Promotion Center, Beijing

Translations by

Richard E. Strassberg

Professor of Chinese, Department of East Asian Languages and Cultures
University of California, Los Angeles

Martha Avery

Presented by

Wonders

The Memphis International Cultural Series
A Division of the City of Memphis, Tennessee
in association with
The State Bureau of Cultural Relics
of the People's Republic of China

This exhibition is sponsored by an indemnity from the Federal Council
on the Arts and the Humanities.

Published by Lithograph Publishing Company,
a division of Lithograph Printing Company

Printed in the United States of America

Library of Congress Catalog Card Number: 95-60723

ISBN 1-882516-04-4 (hardcover)   ISBN 1-882516-05-2 (paperback)

Project Manager: Russ Gordon

Catalogue Production: Curatorial Assistance, Los Angeles
Director: Graham Howe
Editor: Garrett White
Graphic Design: Garrett White, Karen Bowers, Michele Lott
Editorial Staff: Karen Hansgen, Dianne Woo
Production Assistant: Kathleen Tomajan
Photographer: Jeff Veitch

Production Coordinator: Connie Reeves
Color Separations and Printing: Lithograph Printing Company

Paper Provided by INTERNATIONAL PAPER
Cover - Springhill® Bristol, CIS, 12 PT.
Text - 80lb. MIRAWEB™ II Gloss. Contains a minimum 10% post-consumer fiber.
Hardcover End Sheets - 80lb. Beckett Cambric, Ash, Recycled Text

Photography and illustrations courtesy of: Chan Jinghua; China Cultural Relics Promotion Center, 6, 9,
10–11, 12, 13, 15, 58, 59, 60, 61, 63, 64, 65; Dean Conger, © National Geographic Society, 16, 18, 24–25;
Carlos Domenich, 74–75; Fan Shenyan; Gao Yuying; Todd Gipstein, © National Geographic Society, viii–ix, xxxii,
3, 7, 8, 20, 23, 27, 31, 32, 34, 35, 126, 127, 137, 138, 145; Hsien-Min Yang, © National Geographic Image
Collection, 5; Hubei Provincial Museum; Inner Mongolia Institute for Archaeology and Cultural Relics;
Li Fan; Museum of Terracotta Warriors and Horses of Qinshihuang, Shaanxi; James L. Stanfield,
© National Geographic Society, 163; Audrey R. Topping, 17, 29; Wang Lu

Cover: Soul Tower of the Tomb of Huang Tai Ji. Photo by Todd Gipstein, National Geographic Society

CONTENTS

Letter from the Mayor of Memphis

When the City of Memphis established WONDERS: The Memphis International Cultural Series in 1989, our goals for this division were to enhance cultural tourism and to expose as many people as possible to the finest art and culture the world offers. We believe that without an understanding and appreciation of our world's rich history, we cannot venture into the future successfully.

This year, I am pleased to introduce the sixth WONDERS exhibition, "Imperial Tombs of China." More than 250 objects excavated from the tombs of China's most prominent emperors and ancient rulers will be showcased. These objects were carefully selected from twenty-one museums and cultural centers throughout nine Chinese provinces. "Imperial Tombs of China" is the largest exhibition of Chinese tomb treasures ever to come to the United States.

It is significant that as we host this exhibition, the leaders of the American and Chinese governments are establishing a greater sense of cooperation. Cultural exchanges of this magnitude will continue to enhance relationships between our two great nations. I am pleased that you are taking the time to gain a better understanding of Chinese culture through "Imperial Tombs of China." Through this exhibition we celebrate the diversity of the world's peoples and cultures.

Producing an internationally acclaimed exhibition takes a vast amount of time and expertise. I wish to express my sincere appreciation to Ambassadors Zhu Qizhen and Li Daoyu of the People's Republic of China; Sun Wei Xie, Cultural Counselor; Zhang Deqin, Director of the State Bureau of Cultural Relics; and Tong Zhenghong, Director of the Cultural Relics

Promotion Center for their roles in orchestrating this exhibition. Their vision and guidance made this historic exchange a reality.

I also wish to thank the Memphis City Council, The Memphis-Shelby County Port Commission, The State of Tennessee, The Kroger Company, The Coca-Cola Bottling Company of Memphis, Federal Express Corporation, Naegele Outdoor Advertising, Inc., Smith & Nephew Richards Inc., WANG'S International, Inc., and Delta Air Lines. I want especially to recognize and thank Mrs. Mertie Buckman for her generous support. Our two thousand loyal volunteers that give freely of their time to assist our staff in producing this international exhibition also deserve a big thank-you.

Finally, I offer my deep gratitude to Jon Thompson, director of cultural affairs for the City of Memphis. Without Jon's leadership and knowledge of China this exhibition would not have been possible. I also thank the WONDERS staff for their dedication and commitment to this project. Through their efforts, Memphis has received international recognition for innovation in producing blockbuster art exhibitions.

Dr. W. W. Herenton
Mayor
City of Memphis

Letter from the Ambassador of the People's Republic of China

As Ambassador of the People's Republic of China to the United States of America, I am very happy that the United States is the first foreign host of the exhibition "Imperial Tombs of China" with beautiful Memphis as the first stop on its North American tour. It is one of many important projects of friendly cooperation we have enjoyed in various fields. I would like to take this opportunity to extend my best wishes for the success of this exhibition.

We have observed the development and astounding success of WONDERS: The Memphis International Cultural Series since the "Ramesses the Great" exhibition of 1987. This project, unique in the world, brings cultural diversity to the heartland of America. Since China is one of the most ancient civilizations in the world, it is important that Chinese culture be included in this exceptional series.

More than three years of cooperation between the State Bureau of Cultural Relics of China and the City of Memphis have finally culminated in this most significant North American exhibition tour. The anticipated exposure of ancient Chinese culture to millions of American citizens can contribute immeasurably to mutual understanding between our peoples.

Treasures from twenty-one museums and cultural relic repositories in nine provinces throughout China are featured in the exhibition and beautifully preserved in this catalogue. These objects are intended to bring the very best of nearly twenty-five centuries of Chinese cultural history to America, and most particularly, to regions not usually exposed to the depth of our rich cultural heritage.

I am grateful for the diligent efforts of all the people involved in bringing this project to fruition. I sincerely hope that in the future more cultural projects like this exhibition will come to the United States, while the cream of American culture is likewise exposed to the Chinese people.

Li Daoyu
Ambassador Extraordinary and Plenipotentiary
The People's Republic of China to the United States of America

The phenomenon that is WONDERS: The Memphis International Cultural Series continues to amaze, educate, and delight visitors from around the world. We are proud to boast that a WONDERS exhibition is more than an art exhibit, it is a cultural experience! The 1995 production "Imperial Tombs of China" is no exception. "This exhibition," says Wu Xi Hua, Director of the Foreign Affairs Division of the State Bureau of Cultural Relics, "can be said, without a doubt, to be the best that has ever been sent to the States."

Only once in several lifetimes should one be privileged enough to have had the opportunity to associate with the dedicated and talented people, from opposite sides of the world, who produced the incredible results you will enjoy in this exhibition. I remember, fondly, that snowy afternoon three years ago in the Forbidden City, at the offices of the Cultural Relics Promotion Center, State Bureau of Cultural Relics, when we reached agreement in principle on this project. I doubt if Center Director Tong Zhenghong, Professor Lei Congyun, the venerable senior gentleman Xie Chen Sheng, or Associate Professor Yang Yang realized then the complex and arduous journey we would travel to accomplish this objective. But, together, we have achieved.

Assistance from Ambassador Zhu Qizhen and Cultural Counselor Sun Wei Xie, as well as continuous strong support of Ambassador Li Daoyu—all from the Embassy of the People's Republic of China—was invaluable. In Beijing, Zhang Deqin, Director of the State Bureau of Cultural Relics, Zhang Bai, Assistant Director, and Wu Xi Hua were all generous hosts and provided exemplary leadership throughout the negotiations and during the media visit that was the largest to visit China in twenty years. Among my many friends in China, the following individuals also had extremely important roles in bringing this project to fruition: in Xian, Song Zhenxing, Director of the Foreign Affairs Division of the Cultural Relics Bureau of Shaanxi Provincial Government; Wu Yong Qi, Vice Director of the Museum of Terracotta Warriors; Yin Shengping, Vice Curator of the Shaanxi Historical Museum; in Wuhan, Shu Zhi Mei, Director of the Hubei Provincial Museum; and in Shenyang, Sun Mingshan, Director of Cultural Affairs of Shenyang City, and Zhi Yun Ting, Director of the Shenyang Palace Museum.

I will be forever grateful for the unwavering support of Mayor Herenton and the Memphis City Council. The Memphis Shelby County Port Commission provided funding in an unprecedented example of cooperation between unrelated agencies. Our Patrons, Mertie Buckman and Ned Cook, had the vision and generosity to ensure the continuation of the WONDERS series. Their assistance, along with the outpouring of time and treasures from our sponsors and contributors, is an essential part of the successful formula that is WONDERS.

WONDERS exhibitions are known throughout the world for their beautiful architectural settings. Once again, the genius of Louis Pounders has produced a world-class environment that eloquently highlights the treasures without overwhelming them. Finally, thank you to the incredible staff of WONDERS, who have tirelessly given their all to this project, and to our two thousand wonderful volunteers who faithfully return each year to serve their city and the arts. And, a very special thank-you to two brilliant Chinese citizens who have also become close friends: Zhai Zhi Hai and Sheng Wei Wei, who have traveled this adventure with me from the beginning, providing important advice and counsel along with expert interpretation. Most of all, I respect the patience of the Chinese culture they taught me, without which we could never have achieved the results you will witness.

I am very proud to have had a small part in presenting "Imperial Tombs of China" and the rich cultural history of the people of China to the people of America.

Jon K. Thompson

Jon K. Thompson
City of Memphis
Director of Cultural Affairs

Letter from the Director of the State Bureau of Cultural Relics, Beijing

文物以地永恒的光辉照亮人类文明发展的足跡。我確信，美国朋友參覌了中國帝王陵墓展會進一步了解中國，洞察中國人民的心靈。成功與光荣屬於孟菲斯！

一九〇四年十一月 張德勤

Cultural relics, through their eternally brilliant qualities, can reflect the path of development of human civilization. I certainly believe that when our American friends view this exhibition of relics from Chinese imperial tombs, they will gain a deeper understanding of China and the minds and souls of the Chinese people.

This achievement and honor belongs to Memphis!

Zhang Deqin, November 1994

Letter from the Director of the China Cultural Relics Promotion Center, Beijing

"Imperial Tombs of China" is extraordinarily rich in content and the broadest in scope among the great exhibitions of cultural relics that China has sponsored abroad during the past decade. The more than two hundred objects exhibited are cultural treasures selected from twenty-one institutions in nine provinces and cities in China. They are a feast for the eyes that will delight the American people and allow them to thoroughly understand the inexhaustible seductiveness and beauty of Eastern culture. The "Wonders of the World" series of exhibitions in Memphis has already gained widespread fame, and this exhibition of Chinese cultural relics will only increase its brilliant reputation.

I hope that the American people will gain an even greater understanding of ancient Chinese culture. I wish success to the exhibition, "Imperial Tombs of China"!

Tong Zhenghong, November 1994

"中国帝王陵墓展"是近十几年来，中国在海外举办的内涵极其丰富、规模最为宏阔的文物大展。展示在眼前的近三百件展品，是从中国九个省市十七个文博单位遴选出的文物珍品，它将使美国人民一饱眼福，从中领略东方文化的无尽魅力和风彩。美国孟菲斯市的"世界奇观系列展"业已名闻遐迩，此次中国文物展赴美展出，更能为之增辉。

愿美国人民更多地了解中国古代文化。

祝"中国帝王陵墓展"获得成功！

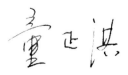

一九九四年十一月四日

PEOPLE'S REPUBLIC OF CHINA ORGANIZING COMMITTEE

Organizer

The State Bureau of Cultural Relics of the People's Republic of China

in association with

The China Cultural Relics Promotion Center

Curators

Lei Congyun, Senior Research Fellow, China Cultural Relics Promotion Center

Yang Yang, Associate Senior Research Fellow, China Cultural Relics Promotion Center

Zhao Gushan, Research Fellow, China Cultural Relics Promotion Center

Planning Committee

Chen Xiaocheng, Wu Xihua, Lei Congyun, Yang Yang

Sheng Wei Wei, Zhang Jianxian, Song Beishan, Zhao Gushan

Additional support provided by

Liang Jinsheng, Zhang Shoushang, Yang Jie

Zhao Giulling, Ye Peilan

LENDERS TO THE EXHIBITION

WONDERS: The Memphis International Cultural Series
expresses its profound gratitude to the following museums and institutions
for the loan of objects for this unprecedented exhibition:

Bureau of Cultural Relics and Gardening of Xian, Shaanxi

China Cultural Relics Promotion Center

China Cultural Relics Coordination Center

Committee for the Preservation of Cultural Relics of Baoding, Hebei

Cultural Relics Administrative Committee of Baoding Prefecture

Cultural Relics Bureau of Xian, Shaanxi

Cultural Relics Excavation Team of Loyang, Henan

Cultural Relics Research Institute of Hebei

Gansu Provincial Museum

Henan Provincial Museum

The Historical Museum of Shaanxi

Hubei Provincial Museum

Inner Mongolia Institute for Archaeology and Cultural Relics

Kuancheng District Museum, Hebei

Loyang Museum, Henan

Museum of Terracotta Warriors and Horses of Qinshihuang, Shaanxi

Nanjing Museum

Palace Museum, Beijing

Shaanxi Provincial Museum of Soldier and Horse Figures
from the tomb of Qinshihuang

Shangqiu City Museum, Henan

Shenyang Palace Museum

WONDERS: THE MEMPHIS INTERNATIONAL CULTURAL SERIES

EXECUTIVE STAFF
Jon K. Thompson, *Executive Director*
Helen "Peachie" Bailey, *Administrative Assistant*

OPERATIONS AND FINANCE
Glen A. Campbell, *Director*
Vernetta Anderson, *Volunteer/Operations Manager*
Kenneson Kyle, *Volunteer/Assistant Manager*
Rebecca Roberson, *Cash Control Manager*
Joseph Wells, *Logistics Coordinator*

MARKETING AND PUBLIC RELATIONS
Twyla Dixon, *Director*
Stacie Shappard, *Secretary*
Kay McDowell, *Public Relations Manager*
Belle Eftink, *Manager, Admissions/Special Events*
Paige Perkins, *Assistant Manager, Admissions/Special Events*
Barbara Gales, *Receptionist*

DESIGN AND CONSTRUCTION
John Conroy, *Deputy City Engineer*
Ron Griffin, *Facility Coordinator*

SECURITY
Major Michael W. Lee, Sr., *Director*
Captain W. D. Merritt, *Assistant Director*
Lieutenant David Booker, *Assistant Director*

CURATORIAL AND EDUCATIONAL SERVICE
Steve Masler, *Chief Curator*
Louella Weaver, *Assistant Curator*

COMMUNITY AND CORPORATE DEVELOPMENT
Narquenta Sims, *Director*
Evangeline Wilson, *Coordinator*

GIFT SHOP
Velma Johnson, *Manager*

INTERNATIONAL CONSULTANT
Amer-China Partners, Inc.
George Bergland
Zhai Zhihai

WONDERS: THE MEMPHIS INTERNATIONAL CULTURAL SERIES

OPERATIONS AND FINANCE
Glen A. Campbell, *Director*

Volunteer Administration
Vernetta Anderson, *Manager*
Kenneson Kyle, *Assistant Manager*
Jean Lamar, *Staff Assistant*

Recorded Tour
Sean Downes, *Manager*
Geraldine Montgomery, *Assistant Manager*
Robert Niederhauser, *Assistant Manager*
Beverly Oliver, *Assistant Manager*
Patrick Perry, *Assistant Manager*
Antenna Theatre
Chris Tellis, *Director of Audio Tours*
Harriet Moss, *Executive Director*
Kathy Baldwin, *Project Manager*
Jessie Boggs, *Writer*
Paul Sagan, *Writer*
Leonard Nimoy, *Narrator*

Exhibition Operations
Vernetta Anderson, *Manager*
Emily Bisso, *Floor Manager*
Peggie Edgmon, *Floor Manager*
Sage Lambert, *Floor Manager*
Timothy Urbanowicz, *Floor Manager*

Catalogue Production
Lei Congyun, *Author, Senior Research Fellow*
Yang Yang, *Author, Associate Senior Research Fellow*
Zhao Gushan, *Author, Research Fellow*

Lithograph Publishing Company, a division of
Lithograph Printing Company
Russ Gordon, *Project Manager*
Connie Reeves, *Production Coordinator*
Vernon Goodner, *Production Coordinator*
David Pinson, *Production Coordinator*
Alan Stevens, *Paper Coordinator*

Curatorial Assistance, Inc., Los Angeles
Graham Howe, *Director*
Garrett White, *Editor*
Karen Bowers, *Graphic Designer*
Karen Hansgen, *Editorial Assistant*
Jeff Veitch, *Photographer*

Insurance
Sedgewick James of Tennessee, Inc.
George Moreland
Chip Moreland
Ken Payler
Allen Insurance Associates
Frederick Schmid

Cash Control
Rebecca Roberson, *Manager*
Angela Louise Hunt, *Assistant Manager*

Video Tour Presentation
Carrcon Productions
Dan Conaway, *Executive Producer*
Wm. Carrier III, *Director*

Art Handling, Transportation, and Installation
Fine Arts Express
Larry Francell
Bruce Lee
Hasenkamp International
Acuff International
Allied Van Lines
Alexander International
LeRoy Pettijohn
Federal Express Corporation
Larry Ashkenaz
Walter McCloughlin

Memphis Cook Convention Center
Morris Fair, *Chairman*
Doug Tober, *General Manager*
Nancy Keathley, *Executive Assistant*
Tom Praise, *Director of Operations*
Declan Mullin, *Operations Manager*

Food Service
Executive Chef Catering
Bruce Scott, *General Manager*
Don Ridley, *Executive Chef*
Lydia McLellan, *Director, Food & Beverages*

MARKETING AND PUBLIC RELATIONS
Twyla Dixon, *Director*
Stacie Shappard, *Secretary*
Kay McDowell, *Public Relations Manager*
Rich Kuzmiak, *Mail Clerk*

Group Sales, Admissions, Special Events
Belle Eftink, *Manager*
Paige Perkins, *Assistant Manager*
Karen Carter, *Supervisor*
Erin Krastins, *Supervisor*
Tony Harley, *Supervisor*
Debbie Pchola, *Supervisor*

Advertising and Marketing
Sossaman, Bateman, McCuddy Advertising, Inc.
Ken Sossaman, *President*
Donna Gordy, *Vice President*
Stephanie Wilson, *Director, Public Relations*
Eric Melkent, *Creative Director*
Beth Graber, *Director, Media Services*
Regina Burns, *Director, Promotions and Community Relations*
Dave Smith, *Copywriter*
Randall Hartzog, *Director, Creative Services*
Daphne Burditt, *Account Coordinator*

Speakers Bureau
Majorie Gerald, *Coordinator*

Visitor Services
Memphis Convention and Visitors Bureau
Kevin Kane, *President*
John Oros, *Vice President, Convention Development*
Regena Bearden, *Director, Tourist Development*
Denise DuBois Taylor, *Director, Communications*
Dorothy Darris, *Director, Information Center*

Tennessee State Department of Tourist Development
The Honorable Sandra Ford Fulton, *Commissioner*
The Honorable John Wade, *Commissioner*

Unique Planning Network
Maudie Kite-Powell, *President*

Communications and Public Relations
Kay McDowell, *Manager*

China Media Trip
Delta Air Lines, Inc.
Nikki Taylor, *District Marketing Supervisor*
Ruth Wood, Peabody Ticket Office
Carol Smith

National Media Luncheon
Elizabeth England, *Consultant*
The Peabody Hotel
Mohamad Hakimian, *General Manager*
Mary Schmitz, *Public Relations Director*
Phil Yankovitch, *Marketing Director*

Grand Inaugural Ceremony
Heartbeat Productions
The Golden Dragon Acrobats
Delta Air Lines, Inc.–Volunteer Team
The Peabody Hotel
Holiday Inn Crowne Plaza
Brownestone Hotel
Hicks Convention Services & Special Events
D. Canale Beverages

Grand Inaugural Gala Events
Jane Work, *Coordinator*
Gala Hall Design
Williamson Haizlip & Pounders, Inc.
Louis Pounders
Brantley Ellzey
Jameson Gibson Construction Company, Inc.
Advance Manufacturing Company
Hicks Convention Services & Special Events
Billy Hicks, *President*
Executive Chef Catering, Food Service

Design and Construction
John Conroy, *Deputy City Engineer*
Ron Griffin, *Facility Coordinator*

Exhibition Design/Architectural Design
Williamson Haizlip & Pounders, Inc.
Louis Pounders, *Architect*

Exhibition Design/Architectural Design *continued*
Clayton Rogers
Brantley Ellzey
Scott Carter
Deanna Gibbs

Case Design and Installation
Quenroe Associates
Elroy Quenroe
Charles Mack

Graphic Design
Robinson Design and Fine Art
Lonnie Robinson

Structural Engineer
Jamnu H. Tahiliani & Associates, Inc.
Jamnu H. Tahiliani

Electrical/Mechanical Engineer
Liles Engineering Design Consultants
James Liles
Ken Shappley

Mountmaker
Robert Fugelstad
Michael Dubé

Exhibition Construction
Jameson-Gibson Construction Company, Inc.
E. P. "Gene" Gibson, Jr., *President*
David L. "Chris" Jameson, *Secretary-Treasurer*
William "Butch" Jenné, Jr., *Superintendent*
John A. Griffin, *Assistant Superintendent*

Advance Manufacturing Company
David A. Craig, *President*
Purvis McAfee, *Superintendent*
Kay Gillis, *Faux Finisher*

Gift Shop
Velma Johnson, *Manager*
Tametrius Reddick, *Assistant Manager*
David Walters, *Inventory Specialist*
WANG'S International, Consultant and Gift Shop Sponsor
Robert Wang, *President and CEO*
Susie Wang, *Chief Operating Officer*
Mary Baker, *Product Director, Specialty Sales*
Gina Campbell, *Manager, Legal Affairs*
Rosa Knichel, *Market Trade Associate*
Carol Cobb McCormack, *Manager,*
Communications & Education
Jerry Shore, *Vice President, Finance*
Linda Sones, *Manager, Specialty Sales Operations*
Chris Sterling, *Manager, Visual Merchandising*

Security
Major Michael W. Lee, Sr., *Director*
Captain W. D. Merritt, *Assistant Director*
Lieutenant David Booker, *Assistant Director*

Security continued
Mr. Frank Tarrance, *Communications*
Mr. Tim Morrow, *Communications*
Interactive Technologies, Inc., *Consultant*

CURATORIAL AND EDUCATIONAL SERVICES
Steve Masler, *Chief Curator*
Louella Weaver, *Assistant Curator*
M. L. Moore, *Exhibition Assistant*

Arts for the Blind and Visually Impaired
Dr. John Hughs, *Coordinator*

Curriculum Guide
Mary Scheuner, *Coordinator*
Rebecca Argall, *Editor*
Wai-Tze Bing, *Text Development*
Darla Linerode, *Text Development*
Lala Cooper, *Text Development*
Lea Ann Flatt, *Text Development*
Tinian Molloy, *Text Development*
Judith Thomoson, *Text Development*
Cassandra Spearman, *Text Development*
Brooke Barnett, *Design*
Pashur House, *Design*
Thor Metzinger, *Design*
David Young, *Calligraphy*
Priscilla Fan, *Calligraphy*
Memphis Art Council, Arts in the School Program
Amellia Barton, *Director*

Docent Training
University of Memphis, Division of Short Courses
Maryann Macdonald, *Lecturer*
Darla Linerode, *Lecturer*
Preston Johnson, *Audio-Visuals*
Memphis Brooks Museum of Art

Introductory Video
The National Geographic Society
Todd Gepstein, *Director of Multi-Image Productions*
Sid Hastings, *Producer, Multi-Image Productions*
Nolans Audio Visuals

Federal Indemnification
National Endowment for the Arts
Federal Council on the Arts and Humanities
Alice M. Whelihan, *Indemnity Administrator*
Sotheby's
Lark E. Mason, Jr., *Vice President of Chinese Works of Art*
The United States Information Agency
Lorie J. Nierenburg, *Assistant General Counsel*

COMMUNITY AND CORPORATE DEVELOPMENT
Narquenta Sims, *Director*
Evangeline Wilson, *Coordinator*
Clifford Stockton, *Advisor*

Imperial Room
Dolphin Garthwright, *Interior Design*
China Town Imports, Furnishings

WONDERS for Children Program
Betty Goff C. Cartwright, *Chairperson*
Jane Holmgrain, *Committee Member*
Betty Hurt, *Committee Member*
Peggy Jones, *Committee Member*
Jane Jones, *Committee Member*
Barbara Perkins, *Committee Member*

CITY OF MEMPHIS
Office of the Chief Administrative Officer
Dave Hansen, *Chief Administrative Officer*
Virginia Wells, *Executive Secretary*
Keenon McCloy, *Administrative Assistant*

Memphis Police Department
Walter J. Winfrey, *Director*
William P. Oldham, *Deputy Director*
Public Relations Crime Unit

Division of Finance and Administration
Rick Masson, *Director*
Roland McElrath, *Deputy Director*
Danny Wray, *Comptroller*
David Crum, *Deputy Comptroller*
Don Morris, *Manager, Accounts Payable*
Lenzie Thomas, *Purchasing Agent*

Division of General Services
Lewis S. Fort, *Director*
Chuck Fox, *Deputy Director*
Darrell Eldred, *Technical Services*
Wesley Arije, *Construction Coordinator*
Buddy Smith, *Supervisor*

Division of Public Works
Benny Lendermon, *Director*
Rodney "Butch" Eder, *Deputy Director*
Gerald Smith, *Supervisor*

Division of Legal Services
Monice Hagler, *City Attorney*
L. Kenneth McCowan, Jr., *Deputy City Attorney*
Russell Hensley, *Assistant City Attorney*

Division of Management and Information Systems
John Hourican, *Director*
Claudia Shumpert, *Administrator*
Delia Bland, *Systems Information*
Tim Guntharp, *Micro Computers*

Division of Engineering
James Collins, *City Engineer*
Paul Cheema, Supervisor, *Traffic Operations*
Larry Johnson, Supervisor, *City Sign Shop*

Division of Personnel
Westelle Florez, *Director*
Bob Bishop, *Manager, Compensation*
Diane Menton, *Manager, Employment*

Sponsors

Patrons

Mertie Buckman

Edward W. Cook

Principal Sponsors

City of Memphis

Coca-Cola Bottling Company of Memphis

Federal Express

The Kroger Company

International Paper

Memphis-Shelby County Port Commission

Naegele Outdoor Advertising, Inc.

Smith & Nephew Richards Inc.

State of Tennessee

WANG'S International

Official Airline

Delta Air Lines, Inc.

MAJOR CONTRIBUTORS

Allied Van Lines

First Tennessee

Motorola

National Endowment for the Arts and Humanities

National Geographic Society

Seessel's Supermarkets

CONTRIBUTORS

Acuff International

Afro-American Police Association

American Society of Training and Development,
Memphis Chapter

Jack Belz

The Brownestone Hotel

D. Canale Beverages

China Town Imports

Christian Brothers High School

The Commercial Appeal

Diversified Employment Services, Inc.

Holiday Inn Crowne Plaza

Hospitality Sales and Marketing Association

Josten's

Junior League of Memphis

LeMoyne-Owen College

Lichterman-Lowenberg Foundation

Lithograph Printing Company

Mayflower Bus Company

Memphis Area Transit Authority

Memphis Arts Council

Memphis Baptist Ministerial Association

Memphis Brooks Museum of Art

Memphis Business Journal

Memphis City Schools

Memphis Convention and Visitors Bureau

Memphis Hotel Managers Association

Memphis International Airport

Memphis Park Commission

Metro Memphis Attractions Association

Mid-South Minority Purchasing Council

National Council of Jewish Women

Radisson Hotel

Victor L. Robilio Co., Inc.

Schering-Plough, Inc.

Sedgewick-James of Tennessee

Shelby County Schools

Southland Chrysler

Tennessee Managed Care Network

The Peabody Hotel

The Tri-State Defender Newspaper

Time Warner Cable System

TRANSAD, Inc.

United States Information Agency

University of Memphis

Volunteer Center of Memphis

WHBQ-TV

WKNO-TV

WMC-TV

WREG-TV

Dynasties

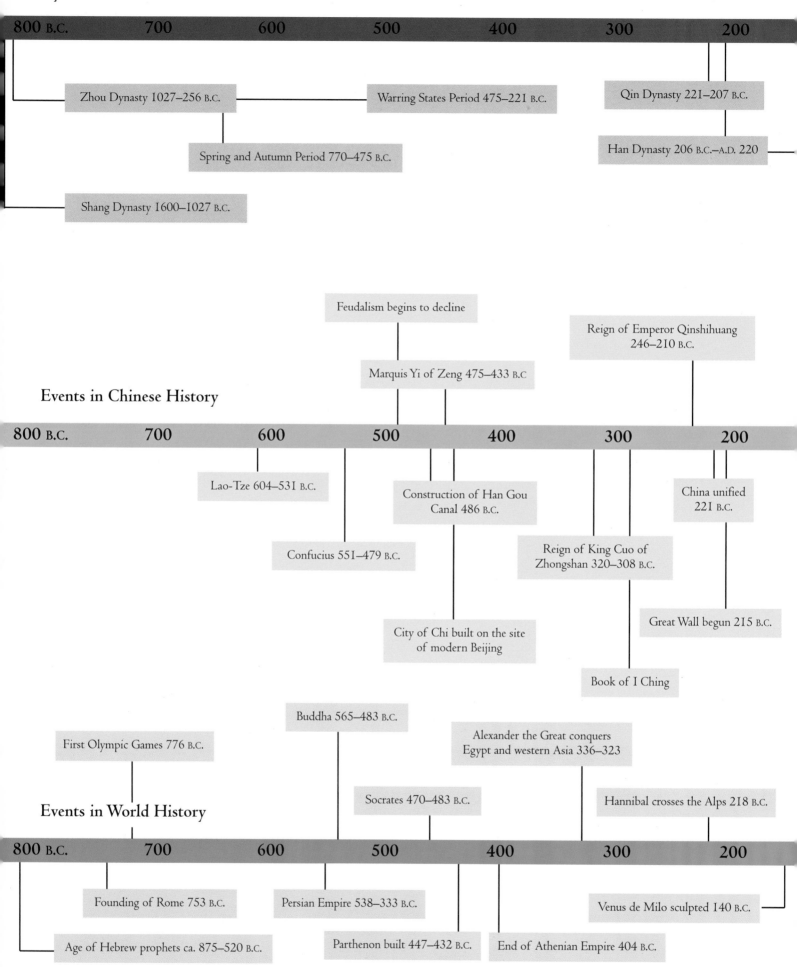

| 800 B.C. | 700 | 600 | 500 | 400 | 300 | 200 |

Zhou Dynasty 1027–256 B.C.

Warring States Period 475–221 B.C.

Qin Dynasty 221–207 B.C.

Spring and Autumn Period 770–475 B.C.

Han Dynasty 206 B.C.–A.D. 220

Shang Dynasty 1600–1027 B.C.

Feudalism begins to decline

Reign of Emperor Qinshihuang
246–210 B.C.

Marquis Yi of Zeng 475–433 B.C

Events in Chinese History

| 800 B.C. | 700 | 600 | 500 | 400 | 300 | 200 |

Lao-Tze 604–531 B.C.

Construction of Han Gou
Canal 486 B.C.

China unified
221 B.C.

Confucius 551–479 B.C.

Reign of King Cuo of
Zhongshan 320–308 B.C.

Great Wall begun 215 B.C.

City of Chi built on the site
of modern Beijing

Book of I Ching

Buddha 565–483 B.C.

First Olympic Games 776 B.C.

Alexander the Great conquers
Egypt and western Asia 336–323

Socrates 470–483 B.C.

Hannibal crosses the Alps 218 B.C.

Events in World History

| 800 B.C. | 700 | 600 | 500 | 400 | 300 | 200 |

Founding of Rome 753 B.C.

Persian Empire 538–333 B.C.

Venus de Milo sculpted 140 B.C.

Age of Hebrew prophets ca. 875–520 B.C.

Parthenon built 447–432 B.C.

End of Athenian Empire 404 B.C.

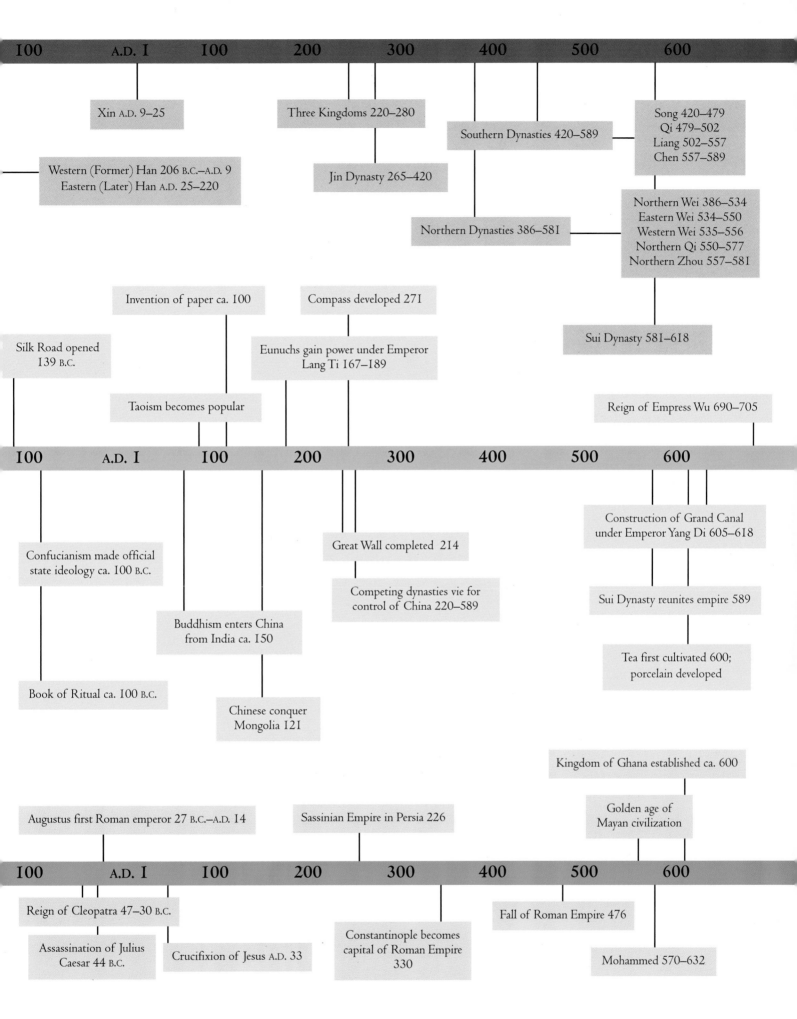

100   A.D. I   **100**   **200**   **300**   **400**   **500**   **600**

Xin A.D. 9–25

Three Kingdoms 220–280

Song 420–479
Qi 479–502
Liang 502–557
Chen 557–589

Southern Dynasties 420–589

Western (Former) Han 206 B.C.–A.D. 9
Eastern (Later) Han A.D. 25–220

Jin Dynasty 265–420

Northern Wei 386–534
Eastern Wei 534–550
Western Wei 535–556
Northern Qi 550–577
Northern Zhou 557–581

Northern Dynasties 386–581

Invention of paper ca. 100

Compass developed 271

Silk Road opened
139 B.C.

Eunuchs gain power under Emperor
Lang Ti 167–189

Sui Dynasty 581–618

Taoism becomes popular

Reign of Empress Wu 690–705

100   A.D. I   **100**   **200**   **300**   **400**   **500**   **600**

Construction of Grand Canal
under Emperor Yang Di 605–618

Great Wall completed 214

Confucianism made official
state ideology ca. 100 B.C.

Competing dynasties vie for
control of China 220–589

Sui Dynasty reunites empire 589

Buddhism enters China
from India ca. 150

Tea first cultivated 600;
porcelain developed

Book of Ritual ca. 100 B.C.

Chinese conquer
Mongolia 121

Kingdom of Ghana established ca. 600

Golden age of
Mayan civilization

Augustus first Roman emperor 27 B.C.–A.D. 14

Sassinian Empire in Persia 226

100   A.D. I   **100**   **200**   **300**   **400**   **500**   **600**

Reign of Cleopatra 47–30 B.C.

Fall of Roman Empire 476

Assassination of Julius
Caesar 44 B.C.

Crucifixion of Jesus A.D. 33

Constantinople becomes
capital of Roman Empire
330

Mohammed 570–632

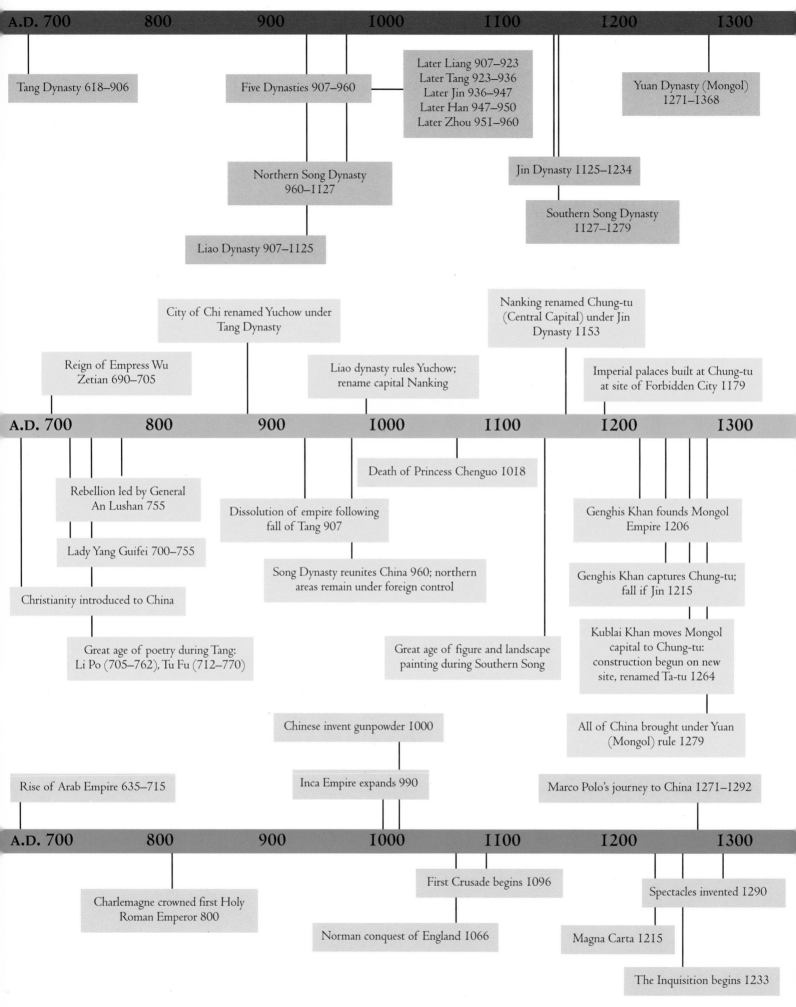

A.D. 700   800   900   1000   1100   1200   1300

Tang Dynasty 618–906

Five Dynasties 907–960

Later Liang 907–923
Later Tang 923–936
Later Jin 936–947
Later Han 947–950
Later Zhou 951–960

Yuan Dynasty (Mongol) 1271–1368

Northern Song Dynasty 960–1127

Jin Dynasty 1125–1234

Southern Song Dynasty 1127–1279

Liao Dynasty 907–1125

City of Chi renamed Yuchow under Tang Dynasty

Nanking renamed Chung-tu (Central Capital) under Jin Dynasty 1153

Reign of Empress Wu Zetian 690–705

Liao dynasty rules Yuchow; rename capital Nanking

Imperial palaces built at Chung-tu at site of Forbidden City 1179

A.D. 700   800   900   1000   1100   1200   1300

Death of Princess Chenguo 1018

Rebellion led by General An Lushan 755

Dissolution of empire following fall of Tang 907

Genghis Khan founds Mongol Empire 1206

Lady Yang Guifei 700–755

Song Dynasty reunites China 960; northern areas remain under foreign control

Genghis Khan captures Chung-tu; fall if Jin 1215

Christianity introduced to China

Kublai Khan moves Mongol capital to Chung-tu: construction begun on new site, renamed Ta-tu 1264

Great age of poetry during Tang: Li Po (705–762), Tu Fu (712–770)

Great age of figure and landscape painting during Southern Song

Chinese invent gunpowder 1000

All of China brought under Yuan (Mongol) rule 1279

Rise of Arab Empire 635–715

Inca Empire expands 990

Marco Polo's journey to China 1271–1292

A.D. 700   800   900   1000   1100   1200   1300

First Crusade begins 1096

Spectacles invented 1290

Charlemagne crowned first Holy Roman Emperor 800

Norman conquest of England 1066

Magna Carta 1215

The Inquisition begins 1233

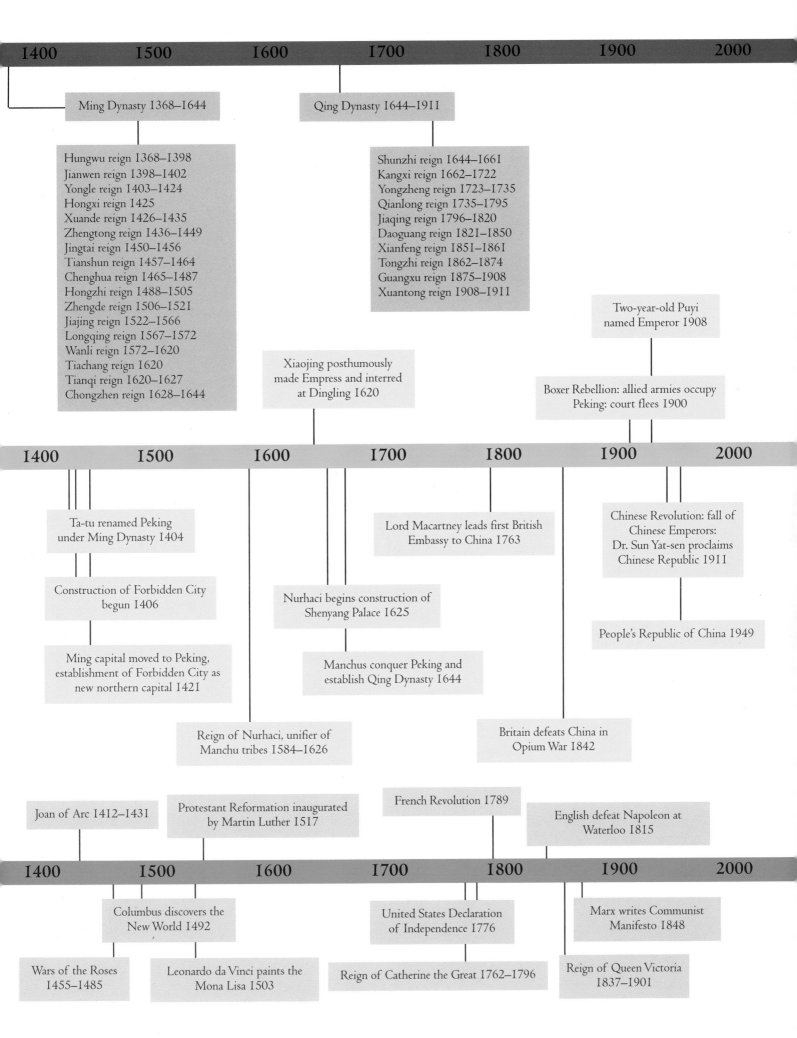

1400   1500   1600   1700   1800   1900   2000

Ming Dynasty 1368–1644

Qing Dynasty 1644–1911

Hungwu reign 1368–1398
Jianwen reign 1398–1402
Yongle reign 1403–1424
Hongxi reign 1425
Xuande reign 1426–1435
Zhengtong reign 1436–1449
Jingtai reign 1450–1456
Tianshun reign 1457–1464
Chenghua reign 1465–1487
Hongzhi reign 1488–1505
Zhengde reign 1506–1521
Jiajing reign 1522–1566
Longqing reign 1567–1572
Wanli reign 1572–1620
Tiachang reign 1620
Tianqi reign 1620–1627
Chongzhen reign 1628–1644

Shunzhi reign 1644–1661
Kangxi reign 1662–1722
Yongzheng reign 1723–1735
Qianlong reign 1735–1795
Jiaqing reign 1796–1820
Daoguang reign 1821–1850
Xianfeng reign 1851–1861
Tongzhi reign 1862–1874
Guangxu reign 1875–1908
Xuantong reign 1908–1911

Two-year-old Puyi
named Emperor 1908

Xiaojing posthumously
made Empress and interred
at Dingling 1620

Boxer Rebellion: allied armies occupy
Peking: court flees 1900

1400   1500   1600   1700   1800   1900   2000

Ta-tu renamed Peking
under Ming Dynasty 1404

Lord Macartney leads first British
Embassy to China 1763

Chinese Revolution: fall of
Chinese Emperors:
Dr. Sun Yat-sen proclaims
Chinese Republic 1911

Construction of Forbidden City
begun 1406

Nurhaci begins construction of
Shenyang Palace 1625

People's Republic of China 1949

Ming capital moved to Peking,
establishment of Forbidden City as
new northern capital 1421

Manchus conquer Peking and
establish Qing Dynasty 1644

Reign of Nurhaci, unifier of
Manchu tribes 1584–1626

Britain defeats China in
Opium War 1842

Joan of Arc 1412–1431

Protestant Reformation inaugurated
by Martin Luther 1517

French Revolution 1789

English defeat Napoleon at
Waterloo 1815

1400   1500   1600   1700   1800   1900   2000

Columbus discovers the
New World 1492

United States Declaration
of Independence 1776

Marx writes Communist
Manifesto 1848

Wars of the Roses
1455–1485

Leonardo da Vinci paints the
Mona Lisa 1503

Reign of Catherine the Great 1762–1796

Reign of Queen Victoria
1837–1901

xxv

Warring States Period

XIONGNU TRIBES

YAN

● Beijing

ZHONGSHAN

ZHAO

● Tomb of
the King of
Zhongshan

HAN

QI

QIN

Yellow River

WEI

Area of
the States
of Song,
Lu, Teng,
and Zou

HAN

ZHOU

Wei River

WEI

● Tomb of
the First
Emperor

Xian

Huai River

CHU

● Tomb of
Marquis Yi

Shanghai ●

SHU

Yangtze River

BA

YUE TRIBES

DIAN TRIBES

● Guangzhou

● Modern cities

Notes on Spelling and Pronunciation

The Chinese speak many dialects. The modern standard dialect and the official language of China is Mandarin, also known as *putonghua*, "the common language." In the *pinyin* system of pronunciation employed throughout this catalogue, the English alphabet represents the sounds of the modern standard dialect. The following initial consonants will help those unfamiliar with the system to read the romanized form of *putonghua*:

Romanized *pinyin* letter	Approximate sound in English
c	au**nts**
q	**ch**ase
x	**sh**e
zh	ur**g**e

Pronunciation guide to Chinese dynasties:

Xia	(sheeah)
Shang	(shahng)
Zhou	(joe)
Qin	(chin)
Han	(hahn)
Xin	(sheen)
Sui	(swee)
Tang	(tahng)
Song	(sawng)
Liao	(leeyow)
Yuan	(yuwahn)
Ming	(meeng)
Qing	(cheeng)

Chronology of Dynasties

Neolithic Period
5000–2000 B.C.	Yanshao Culture
3000/2500–1500 B.C.	Longshan Culture
2000–1500 B.C.	Xia Dynasty

Shang Dynasty
1600–1027 B.C.

Zhou Dynasty
1027–771 B.C.	Western Zhou
770–256 B.C.	Eastern Zhou
770–475 B.C.	Spring and Autumn Period
475–221 B.C.	Warring States Period

Qin Dynasty
221–207 B.C.

Han Dynasty
206 B.C.–A.D. 9	Western (Former) Han
A.D. 9–25	Xin
25–220	Eastern (Later) Han

Three Kingdoms
220–280

Jin Dynasty
265–420

Northern Dynasty
386–534	Northern Wei
534–550	Eastern Wei
535–556	Western Wei
550–577	Northern Qui
557–581	Northern Zhou

Southern Dynasty
420–479	Song
479–502	Qi
502–557	Liang
557–589	Chen

Sui Dynasty
581–618

Tang Dynasty
618–906

Five Dynasties
907–923	Later Liang
923–936	Later Tang
936–947	Later Jin
947–950	Later Han
951–960	Later Zhou

Liao Dynasty
907–1125

Northern Song Dynasty
960–1127

Southern Song Dynasty
1127–1279

Jin Dynasty
1115–1234

Yuan Dynasty (Mongol)
1271–1368

Ming Dynasty
1368–1398	Hungwu reign
1398–1402	Jianwen reign
1403–1424	Yongle reign
1425	Hongxi reign
1426–1435	Xuande reign
1436–1449	Zhengtong reign
1450–1456	Jingtai reign
1457–1464	Tianshun reign
1465–1487	Chenghua reign
1488–1505	Hongzhi reign
1506–1521	Zhengde reign
1522–1566	Jiajing reign
1567–1572	Longqing reign
1572–1620	Wanli reign
1620	Tiachang reign
1620–1627	Tianqi reign
1628–1644	Chongzhen reign

Qing Dynasty
1644–1661	Shunzhi reign
1662–1722	Kangxi reign
1723–1735	Yongzheng reign
1735–1795	Qianlong reign
1796–1820	Jiaqing reign
1821–1850	Daoguang reign
1851–1861	Xianfeng reign
1862–1874	Tongzhi reign
1875–1908	Guangxu reign
1908–1911	Xuantong reign

Forbidden City

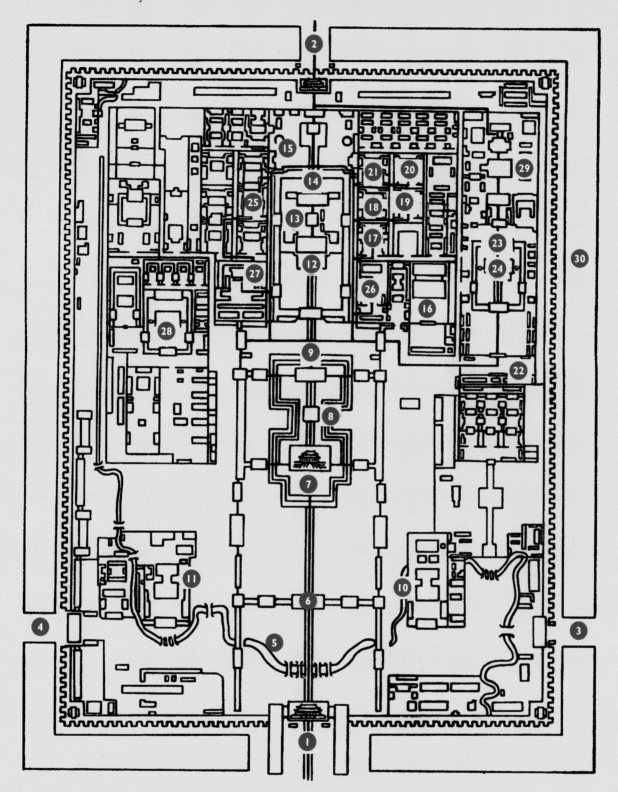

Near the city of Shenyang, the first Qing capital, stands the soul tower of the tomb of the second Qing ruler, Huang Tai Ji.

On Ancient Imperial Mausoleums of China

by Lei Congyun

The mausoleums of China's kings, emperors, and aristocrats represent an extremely important cultural phenomenon, an essential element in our understanding of Chinese history. Whether our knowledge of imperial mausoleums and their contents comes from archaeological studies or ancient texts, burial practices richly define the characteristics of an era.

China's long history—the oldest continuous civilization on Earth—has included innumerable kingdoms and dynasties, and the tombs of its rulers have been widely distributed throughout the land. These historical sites occupy extensive areas, were built on a large scale, and are distinctive in terms of design and architecture. Archaeological evidence of burial practices in China shows a religious awareness, a concept of the soul, from the earliest stages of primitive society. Nearly half a million years ago, the people living in hillside caves at Zhoukoudian, outside modern Beijing, buried their dead in the immediate vicinity of their homes. They sprinkled powdered hematite (red iron ore) over the bodies, and included in the burial pieces of flint, stone tools, and simple ornaments such as stone beads and pierced animal teeth.

Humans appear to have formed the practice of burying objects with the dead at almost the same time a conscious approach to burial emerged. Over the centuries, an increase in the quantity of burial objects paralleled a change in attitudes brought on by increased production in the latter stages of clan society. Still later, burial of the highest rulers of China's Shang and Zhou dynasties (ca. seventeenth–eleventh century B.C., and ca. eleventh–221 B.C., respectively) included large numbers of live human offerings or human sacrifices, along with large quantities of funerary objects, so that burials came to have complex and ornate rites associated with them. By the time of the Han dynasty (206 B.C.–A.D. 220), the practice of human sacrifice had ceased, replaced by the custom of burying ceramic and wood figures to represent those who would have been forced to accompany their master in death.

The Chinese tradition of elaborate burial sought to establish a realm in which "death approximates life." China's kings and emperors wanted their final resting places to rival or even surpass palace architecture in magnificence and opulence. Consequently, these resting places were filled with a wealth of elegant burial objects that today have become rare cultural relics. The fourth-century B.C. Confucian philosopher Xunzi wrote, "In the funeral rites one adorns the dead as though they were still living and sends them to the grave with forms of symbolic life. They are treated as though dead, and yet as though still alive, as though gone and yet as though still present. Beginning and end are thereby unified."

In ancient Chinese texts, the word *mu* ("grave") is synonymous with the word *mo* ("no longer existing"). That is, when a person died, he was buried underground and was no more. For a long time in China, there was no practice of building a mound over a tomb, no visible commemoration of the deceased. From what we know of archaeological remains, supplemented by references in ancient texts, imperial and aristocratic tombs went through several general stages of development: from a vertical shaft in the earth lined with wooden planks, to an earthen pit with wooden planks, to a stone-lined pit, to an arched stone tomb, and finally to an arched underground complex made of stone. This underground complex is called the "dark palace" (*xuangong*) or "secluded palace" (*yougong*). Because of their elaborate construction and beautiful furnishings, comparable to the palaces of living emperors, dark palaces have also commonly been described as "underground palaces."

The practice of building a mound over a tomb probably began during the Xia (ca. twenty-second–seventeenth century B.C.) and Shang dynasties. With the advent of mounds came the building of architectural structures over the mounds. In Anyang, Henan province, for example, the thirteenth-century B.C. tomb of Fu Hao, wife of King Wu Ding (r. ca. 1200–1181 B.C.), was excavated at the Shang dynasty site known as Yinxu. From traces in the earth at its entrance and nearby, it appears that a building was once erected over the tomb. Buried in her tomb were 1,928 jade and bronze objects. Also found were the remains of at least sixteen sacrificed humans.

Historical records show that by the beginning of the Zhou dynasty the piling of both large and small grave mounds over tombs was widespread. According to the *Book of Ritual* (*Liji*), the Confucian classic describing proper ritual ceremonies of Zhou dynasty China, a man's rank should be the measure of the hill that covers him. In other words, the office a man held in society should determine the size of his burial mound.

During the Spring and Autumn and Warring States periods (770–221 B.C.), the height of grave mounds and the size of the buildings over graves grew even larger. The scale and form of royal and aristocratic tombs were modeled on mountains, so that some tombs of kings and aristocrats came to be known as "mounts." For example, the tomb of King Wuling of Zhao (r. 325–299 B.C.) is known as Mount Zhao. In addition to building imposing mounds of earth over their tombs, China's kings and emperors eventually began to build funerary parks around their tomb sites. Later developments included a Sacred Way leading up to the tombs, symbolic guards of honor carved in stone, and various buildings to house the tomb's keepers. The design of a tomb and its environs often resembled a vast, walled city.

Generations of emperors have made the preservation of their ancestral tombs one of the major tasks of the imperial family. This was due to the belief that the ancestors had souls and could help guard and protect their domains. At the same time, caring for the tombs was a means of expressing gratitude to ancestors for their beneficence and virtue. The protection and management of imperial tombs was already systematized by the time of the Western Han dynasty (206 B.C.–A.D. 9), so that the empty land where an emperor was to be buried was intentionally developed into a prosperous area. On the outskirts of the Han dynasty capital, Chang'an, for example, were the mausoleums of Emperor Gaozu (r. 206–195 B.C.), Emperor Hui (r. 195–188 B.C.), Emperor Jing (r. 154–141 B.C.), Emperor Wu (r. 141–87 B.C.), and Emperor Zhao

Beyond the tomb's soul tower lies the burial mound of the second Qing ruler, Huang Tai Ji (r. 1626–1643). Huang Tai Ji—eighth son of the first Qing ruler, Nurhaci—was close to conquering the Ming capital when he died at fifty-two. The capture of Beijing was left to his half-brother, Dorgon, who established Qing rule there under his nephew, Shunzhi (r. 1644–1661).

(r. 87–74 B.C.). The area surrounding them became five thriving "tomb counties." Later dynasties were similarly strict about preserving imperial tombs.

In the tomb of the Warring States era ruler King Cuo of Zhongshan (r. ca. 320–308 B.C.), discovered in Pingshan district, Hebei province, in 1974, a bronze plaque was found engraved with an elaborate site plan for the king's burial park. Although partially looted in antiquity, the tomb and surrounding sacrificial pits still held objects—examples of which are included in this exhibition—that demonstrate the excess of the king's vision for a funerary monument befitting his royal status. The park, unfinished at the time of the king's death, would have included five above-ground pavilions for the king and his wives and concubines. Architectural renderings based on dimensions taken from the bronze plaque reveal

the planned burial ground to have been a precursor to the colossal funerary park of the First Emperor, Qinshihuang.

Qinshihuang (r. 246–210 B.C.), the Qin state ruler who conquered the six other Warring States and unified China in 221 B.C., loved to celebrate his accomplishments. While engaging hundreds of thousands of conscripts to build the Great Wall and other immense construction projects, the emperor is said to have forced 700,000 laborers to build a tomb for him of unprecedented grandeur. Begun after the king's ascension to the throne at the age of thirteen, the tomb was still unfinished forty years later at the fall of the Qin capital in 206 B.C., four years after the emperor's death.

Seen from a distance, the tomb looked like a towering mountain pulled up out of the earth in the shape of a giant upside-down dipper. The four-sided rammed-earth construction was

Following the unification of China—"all under heaven"—by First Emperor Qinshihuang, one tenth of the population was conscripted to fulfill his vast construction plans. It is said that 700,000 laborers were put to work on the emperor's 22-square-mile necropolis at Lishan.

originally almost 400 feet in height, and wider at the bottom than at the top. The base of the mound has a circumference of 1.29 miles. This type of grave mound, with a square-shaped upper section and flat top, has become known as a "flat-top tomb." From both textual records and archaeological remains, it appears that flat-top tombs continued to be popular during the succeeding Han dynasty (206 B.C.–A.D. 220), and were still being used well into the Song dynasty (960–1279).

Two "city walls" were built around the perimeter of the grave mound of Qinshihuang. The inner wall had a circumference of 2.4 miles, the outer a circumference of 3.85 miles. The rammed-earth foundations of the walls were 26 feet wide. Palace-style pavilions were built within the walls, and the ground where they once stood is still covered with the rubble of ancient tiles.

In "Basic Annals of Qin" in the *Historical Records (Shiji*: "Qin benji"), it is written that after the death of the emperor the rulers of Qin were afraid that the artisans constructing the tombs would reveal the secrets of the underground palace. "When the work was done, after the great event, and after everything was hidden away in its rightful place, the inner door was shut and then the outer door was lowered into place. All the craftsmen and laborers were shut inside, and none was allowed out again." To prevent anyone from pillaging the tomb, "craftsmen built devices within it that would set off arrows should anyone pass through the tunnels."

It is said that the treasures buried with Qinshihuang were too numerous to count, that his corpse was covered by a shroud made of pearls and jade, and that his body was clothed in a suit of jade pieces sewn together with gold thread. According to historical records, a representation of the heavens and a topographical map were built into the tomb. The sun and moon were represented by luminescent pearls that shone day and night; rivers and oceans were depicted by streams and pools of mercury. But sources also state that the First Emperor's tomb was looted for thirty days at the fall of the dynasty. Since the underground palace has not yet been excavated, we can only guess at what may lie within.

Nevertheless, abundant archaeological evidence from nearby areas leaves no doubt about the magnificent wealth buried with Qinshihuang. In 1976, three pits were discovered approximately one mile east of the tomb mound. These pits contain Qinshihuang's spectacular burial guard, an army of 8,000 life-sized terracotta warriors, chariots, and horses. Five of these life-sized and intensely lifelike horses and warriors are included in this exhibition, along with bronze weapons once held by the warriors.

While flat-top tombs continued to be built centuries after the death of Qinshihuang, others had begun to use an existing mountain or hill as the site of their tombs. For example, the Western Han tomb of Liu Sheng, Prince Jing of Zhongshan, and his wife, discovered at Mancheng, Hebei province, was built into a mountain, the mountain itself serving as the grave mound.

The practice of using a mountain as a natural tomb reached its height during the Tang dynasty (618–907). Examples include the tomb

The Dingling tomb of the Wanli emperor (r. 1572–1620) is one of thirteen Ming dynasty imperial tombs located in a 15.6-square-mile funerary park near Beijing. The tomb's most prominent feature is the "square citadel and soul tower." Behind the yellow-roofed tower is the circular "city wall and dome" area above the underground palace that contains the emperor's coffin.

of Emperor Taizong of the Tang (r. 626–649) at Zhaoling, and the joint tomb of Emperor Gaozong of the Tang (r. 649–683) and Empress Wu (r. 684–704), buried together at Qianling. Not only was this burial method of "using a mountain for a grave instead of building a tomb" difficult for human labor to match in magnificence and grandeur, it could also far better represent the spirits of kings and emperors.

By the Ming and Qing dynasties (1368–1644 and 1644–1911, respectively), the form in which tombs were constructed came to be known as "city wall and dome" (*baocheng baoding*). More than thirty imperial tombs in Beijing and in the districts of Hebei and Liaoning and more than one hundred imperial consort tombs are of

this type. The Ming tombs are mostly round, while those from the Qing dynasty are oblong.

These tombs were constructed by building a high brick wall above ground around the perimeter of an underground palace. Inside this brick wall was a rounded dome or mound built of rammed earth that towered over the top of the surrounding wall, which was finished with crenellations and small holes. This form gave the tomb the appearance of a small city. In front of the wall, a square walled terrace was raised on which a tower was constructed. This section of the tomb was called "the square citadel and soul tower" (*fangcheng minglou*). This "square citadel and soul tower," together with the "city wall and dome," formed a single architectural unit. Inside the tower stood a stone tablet, or stele, on which

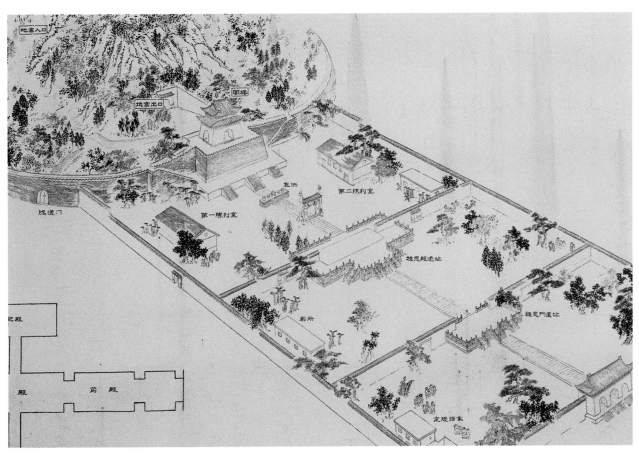

Imperial tombs were the sites of many important rituals performed by living emperors who believed that the welfare of their empires relied on the beneficence of their ancestors. Places for sacrifice, such as the ceremonial arch and "Five Stone Offerings" at the base of the soul tower, are located in the rectangular park (*above*) leading to the Wanli emperor's underground palace.

was inscribed the posthumous titles of the deceased emperor or empress. Altogether, this new and more artistically evolved form of architecture, which combined "city wall and dome" with "square citadel and soul tower," expressed more effectively than the flat-top style the majestic power required of an imperial tomb.

Although certain styles of architecture and construction persisted for centuries, many aspects of tomb architecture have evolved with the tastes and traditions of China's dynasties. For example, earlier main buildings always included a hall for sacrifices and living quarters for the tomb's attendants, whereas the Sacred Way and the symbolic guard of honor were added later.

The thirteen tombs of the Ming dynasty occupy 15.6 square miles, rivaling anything constructed for the living. The tombs are located in Changping district, in Beijing, and lie at the foot of the Tianshou Mountains. Around the tombs is a 7.4-mile wall studded with ten entrances and guard towers where soldiers were stationed to protect the tombs. The tomb area is entered through the Great Red Gate and a stone memorial archway. Facing south, the Great Red Gate has three arched openings and is constructed of stone and brick atop a white stone foundation. The archway, 110 feet wide and 34.4 feet high, is supported by six pillars and covered with a palace-style roof.

Northeast of the gate is a building known as the Hall for Shaking Off the Dust of the World (*Fuchendian*). This was where living emperors changed their clothes before proceeding

Ruler of the Warring States era state of Zeng, Marquis Yi (d. 433 B.C.) was buried in two coffins, an outer coffin made of wood and bronze and an inner wooden coffin. The inner wooden coffin was found damaged by water seepage, but a model (*above*) reproduces the elaborate lacquerwork that adorned the original. Excavated in 1978 at Leigudun, Hubei province (*opposite and overleaf*), the tomb contained more than ten tons of bronze artifacts, the most ever found at a Chinese burial site.

to make sacrificial offerings to the emperors who came before them.

North of the Great Red Gate is the Sacred Way, which stretches 3,477 feet and leads to Changling, the largest of the Ming Tombs. Along this north-to-south passageway are:

- a ceremonial archway covering a stele that reads, "The Divine Merit and Sacred Virtue of the Changling Mausoleum of the Great Ming Dynasty."
- a stone pillar.
- eighteen facing pairs of lifelike stone carvings of animals and human figures. These include lions, mythical beasts known as *xiezhai* and *qilin*, camels, elephants, two pairs of horses (one standing and one kneeling in each pair), and twelve human figures, including civil, military, and meritorious officials (four in each category). Each of these statues is carved from a large single piece of white marble.

- Gate of the Ling Star (*Lingxingmen*), which is a ceremonial stone arch.

The immediate precinct of each Ming tomb also has a surrounding wall. At the gate of each tomb is a blank stone tablet. It is said that these wordless tablets were meant to indicate that the most enduring deeds of emperors would be judged later by those who were still alive.

Within the walls of each tomb are the Gate of the Benevolent Soul (*Ling'enmen*) and the Hall of the Benevolent Soul (*Ling'endian*). The latter was used for making sacrifices before the tomb and was quite large, composed of three or five bays flanked by corridors. Behind this hall is a ceremonial arch and "Five Stone Offerings." These five offerings rest on a table carved from stone, beneath which is a representation of the sacred Buddhist mountain, Mount Sumeru. The "Five Stone Offerings" are placed on the table; in the center is a stone incense burner, on either side of

The underground palace of the Dingling tomb of the Ming dynasty emperor Zhu Yijun (1563–1620), known as the Wanli emperor, is the only imperial tomb to have been scientifically excavated. Three coffins containing the bodies of the emperor and his two empresses, Xiaoduan and Xiaojing, were found surrounded by twenty-nine treasure-filled red lacquer chests.

which are two stone candleholders and a pair of stone vases. Beyond this set of offerings is the square citadel and soul tower. The soul tower is tall and square with double eaves, below which hangs a placard engraved with the name of the tomb. Inside the soul tower is an erect stele, on which is engraved the temple and posthumous names of the emperor.

The city wall and dome of the Changling tomb has a diameter of 1,115 feet. Its Hall of the Ling Star (*Lingxingdian*) is surrounded by three tiers of marble balustrades. The hall is nine bays wide and five bays deep, with double eaves and a covered top. The hall covers 21,000 square feet

and is supported by thirty-two massive pillars, 3.3 feet in diameter, made of the fragrant, durable hardwood known as *nanmu*. The city wall and dome, at the back of the tomb area, is a great rammed-earth mound, below which are the emperor's and empresses' actual resting places. To the right and left of the tomb are a number of subsidiary buildings once used by officials and guards.

The Ming dynasty Dingling tomb of the Wanli Emperor is the only imperial underground palace to have been scientifically excavated. Zhu Yijun, the Wanli emperor (r. 1572–1620), personally selected the site for his tomb and

The Wanli emperor, who ascended the throne at the age of nine and reigned for nearly half a century, followed the custom of supervising the construction of his own tomb, which required the labor of 30,000 workers and cost the equivalent of two years of national land tax revenues. Boots and remnants of clothing surrounding the emperor's remains show his reputedly large size.

oversaw every detail of its construction, which required eighteen years to complete.

On September 19, 1959, after entering the main passageway, opening the "diamond-hard wall" (*jin'gangqiang*), and passing through a tunnel and several stone doors, archaeological workers entered the underground palace of the Dingling tomb. The primary architectural components of the tomb were the passageway and underground palace. The passageway was composed of a gate leading into a brick passageway and then a stone passageway, ending at the "diamond-hard wall." The gate, located at an arched entrance on the south side of the city wall and dome, was where

the coffins of the Wanli emperor and his empresses, Xiaoduan and Xiaojing, were brought into the tomb. The brick passageway was 14.7 feet high, 26.2 feet wide, and 162.3 feet long. The stone passageway, constructed of veined stones, was 131.2 feet long. The diamond-hard wall at the end of the stone passage was 28.8 feet high and 5.2 feet thick. The underground palace was composed of an antechamber, a central chamber, a rear chamber, and left and right flanking chambers.

Antechamber: At the end of the arched tunnel is a great stone gate with two stone doors. Each door is 10.8 feet high and 5.6 feet wide and carved from a single piece of marble. Studs and carved animal heads protrude from the lustrous surface. The antechamber is a rectangular room with an arched stone ceiling. It measures 65.6 feet in length, 19.7 feet in width, and 23.6 feet in height, and is paved with square bricks.

Central chamber: This chamber has an arched gateway and stone gate similar to those of the antechamber. The room is 105 feet long, 19.6 feet wide, and 23.6 feet high, and is also paved with bricks.

Rear chamber: This is the main room of the underground palace and contained the coffins of the emperor and empresses. It measures 98.7 feet in length, 29.8 feet in width, and 31 feet in height. The floor is paved with impeccably cut and fitted veined stone polished to a sheen.

Left and right flanking chambers: In each of these chambers, which flank the central chamber, are platforms that served as "beds" or resting places for coffins, and "gold wells" (*jinjing*) that are identical in shape and construction.

Together, the underground palace and passageway are 286.4 feet in length and 155 feet across, and cover 12,858 square feet. The city wall and dome and underground palace constitute the main architecture of the mausoleum, and from conception to execution they form an integrated whole. The material used for the foundations, balustrades, bridges, canals, and docks above ground was stone throughout and included white marble and veined stone. The wood used was primarily *nanmu*. The main buildings, including the Gate of the Ling Star, the Hall of the Ling Star, and the soul tower, were also constructed of wood and stone and had yellow-glazed tiles, vermilion walls, and carved and painted roof beams. Magnificent palaces in their own right, these buildings succeeded in creating a realm in which death could approximate life.

The excavation of the Dingling tomb has provided a relatively complete picture of the circumstances of a Ming dynasty imperial burial. The organization and description of the objects accompanying the burial of the Wanli emperor are as follows: There was nothing in the left and right flanking chambers in the underground palace. In the central chamber were the memorial tablets of the emperor and empresses, as well as five stone sacrificial articles and an eternal lamp. Burial goods were placed mainly inside the coffins and in "treasure trunks" at the northern and southern ends of the coffin platforms in the rear chamber. Altogether, there were 2,648 objects. These included silk fabrics and garments, gold and silver objects, jades, ceramics, headdresses, crowns, belts, ornaments, bronze and tin funerary objects, lacquer ware, and wooden figurines.

On top of the coffins lay ritual objects such as spears, halberds, axes, and swords. There were four rings of jade (*jue*) at both the northern and southern ends of each coffin and one ring to the east. An incense burner, a vase, and gold and silver ingots lay just to the north of the coffin of the Wanli emperor; a small wooden cart and sedan stood on a platform to the north of the coffin of the Empress Xiaoduan.

In the back chamber, weapons such as swords, bows and arrows, a bow container, an arrow container, and other wooden funerary objects were set in the northwest corner. In the

The coffin of Empress Xiaoduan was opened during the 1958 excavation of the Wanli emperor's tomb, revealing the empress's ornate headdress (*above*). Nearby was the coffin of Empress Xiaojing, originally a concubine who bore the emperor's first son.

northeast corner were red-lacquered square wooden trays and household funerary objects, including a wooden table, a square bench, a basin holder, a screen, and dishes. Four trunks containing wooden figures were placed by the eastern wall. Wooden household articles and two iron lanterns were placed by the north wall. By the south wall were many types of food containers that seem to have been meant for the emperor and empresses. In addition, there were twenty-nine trunks of objects accompanying the burial, twenty-two of which were on the ceremonial platform and seven of which were placed to the north of the coffins.

The large number of burial objects in the Dingling tomb was matched only by the variety of their purposes. There were weapons for the guards of honor, daily necessities, art objects, writing utensils, even objects illustrating accomplishments in science and technology, all of which have yielded data for the study of politics, economy, culture, burial practices, and fashion in the late Ming period.

The phoenix crown of the Ming imperial concubine—Empress Xiaojing—and other dazzling objects displayed in this exhibition demonstrate the wealth and sophistication of Ming dynasty rulers.

The present exhibition displays objects from imperial and aristocratic tombs dating from the Bronze Age Warring States period to the Qing era, the last of China's imperial dynasties. The earliest objects are from the tomb of Marquis Yi, ruler of the small state of Zeng, who was buried in 433 B.C. The tomb, located in Sui district, Hubei

The sacrificial chamber of the Wanli emperor's underground palace (*above*) contained carved marble thrones and a blue-and-white urn—"everlasting lamp"—that once held a wick afloat in sesame oil, burned to nourish the spirits of the emperor and his wives. The posthumous names of the emperor and empresses were inscribed on a stone stele (*opposite*) in the tomb's soul tower.

province, held 15,404 burial objects made of bronze, lacquer, lead and tin, leather, gold, jade, bamboo, silk, hemp, and ceramic. These included ritual vessels, musical instruments, weapons and armor, objects for use with horses and chariots, and articles for daily use. The most extraordinary find was a set of 65 bronze bells weighing 5,500 pounds. Altogether, more than ten tons of bronze artifacts were excavated. Artifacts in this exhibition include bronze cooking vessels (*ding*), wine containers (*zun* and *hu*), a set of chimes with a bronze rack (*bianqing*), and other ritual vessels.

More than ten thousand items were excavated from the Warring States tomb of King Cuo of Zhongshan in Pingshan district, Hebei. Among the extraordinarily graceful objects

excavated were many types of bronze weapons and containers, brilliant silver and gold objects, exquisitely carved jade, a bronze table inlaid with gold and silver that the king would have used in his work, and a tent for travel—anything the king might have needed in life was provided. Objects included in this exhibition from the tomb of the King of Zhongshan include a gold- and silver-inlaid pedestal in the shape of a tiger devouring a deer, a winged mythical creature, bronze halberds, and bronze ritual vessels. In light of their size, magnificent modeling, and detailed workmanship, these bronzes are exceedingly rare.

These artifacts reflect the rituals, musical styles, hunting and military practices, styles of decorative design, culinary traditions, and daily necessities of the time.

The tomb of the Ming dynasty Wanli emperor is entered through an archway once sealed by massive marble slabs.

Chinese Emperors

by Yang Yang

China is a country of ancient history, immense territory, and diverse peoples. The ancestors of the Chinese settled on the east Asian continent at least 10,000 years ago. Within a century of its founding in the twenty-second century B.C., the Xia dynasty was operating as a state and showed an emerging stratification of society. China became a unified national entity in 221 B.C., and would then experience more than 2,000 years of imperial rule.

The first head of state in the Xia dynasty was Qi, son of the Great Yu. Qi was given the title *Hou*. Historical texts generally refer to him as *Xia Hou*, or *Xia Hou Shi*, "Head of the Xia Clan." This followed the same practice of addressing the head of a clan as in earlier, less developed societies. The Xia dynasty lasted for about 400 years. After its overthrow by Tang of the Shang, the Shang dynasty was established (ca. seventeenth–eleventh century B.C.). The Shang leaders felt that they were no longer mere local chieftains but rather the rulers of everything under heaven. The term *Hou* was now inappropriate. From the time of Tang of the Shang, the head of state was called *Wang*, or "King."

Succeeding the Shang, the Zhou dynasty (ca. eleventh century–221 B.C.) also addressed its head of state as king. The domain over which King Zhou ruled was known as "all under heaven." It was said that "nothing under heaven lies outside the lands of the king, and all who rule those lands are the subjects of the king." The Zhou king was also called the "Son of Heaven." This signified that the eldest son of heaven had been invested by heaven with the power to govern mankind.

In 246 B.C., Ying Zheng came to the throne as King Zheng of Qin, the strongest of the seven Warring States. In 221 B.C., at the age of thirty-eight, the king brought an end to the Warring States period, during which China had been divided among fighting aristocratic clans. He united these kingdoms, setting up a great empire with a high degree of centralized power. One of the first major actions he took after unifying China was to change the name by which the head of state was addressed. Following discussions with his ministers and learned advisors, King Zheng finally decided to adopt the title *Huangdi*, "Emperor," and was known thereafter as Qinshihuang.

In bronze inscriptions, the character *Huang* means "resplendent, beautiful, and grand." *Di* originally signified "God in Heaven," or "the Highest Power"—the dominant god ruling over the myriad things in the universe and above whom none is higher. But these words also had other, more specific meanings. By the Warring States period, a traditional concept of the "Three Huang and Five Di" was well established. The Three Huang were the emperors of Heaven, Earth, and Man; the Five Di were Huangdi, Zhuanxu, Diku, Yao, and Shun. The legendary Five Di were mythical emperors who by the time of Qinshihuang had been canonized by Confucian philosophers as sage, ideal rulers and cultural heroes from a golden age in the past. Since Qinshihuang felt that his moral standing was equal to the Three Huang, and that his deeds had

The Inner Golden River winds across the Forbidden City's Great Courtyard of the Gate of Supreme Harmony. The river is spanned by five marble bridges symbolizing the five virtues. The central bridge could only be crossed by the emperor. Beyond the Gate of Supreme Harmony lies the monumental Hall of Supreme Harmony, which was the center of court activities.

already surpassed the Five Di, he put them together and made *Huangdi* his imperial title.

The difference between this new title and the previous one of *king* was that sacred and temporal powers were now brought together in one person. The result was government by an absolute ruler whose status was insurmountable. From that time forward, until the Xinhai Revolution overthrew the Qing dynasty in 1911, the title *Huangdi* applied to the rulers of China.

The emperor had descended from heaven to rule the world, so his power was absolute. He was the "True Dragon Son of Heaven" and first of all men under heaven. In order to give the respect due this title, a whole set of rules were developed with regard to how the person of the emperor should be addressed. The word *zhen* was originally an ordinary pronoun for the first person singular. But from the time of Qinshihuang, only the emperor was allowed to use this way of saying "I." Similarly, "Son of Heaven" was an address that could be applied only to the emperor.

The term *wansui*, "ten thousand years" or "long life," was originally used by common people during celebrations. During the Qin and Han dynasties, this phrase was often used when ministers appeared in court before the emperor to ask for his beneficence and to celebrate his virtues. Thus, the phrase became a symbolic way of referring to the emperor.

The term *bixia* originally meant the ministers and officials who stood guard at the foot of the stairs leading to the emperor's hall. Those waiting to talk with the Son of Heaven but not daring to address him directly for fear of showing disrespect would ask these intermediaries to transmit their messages. As a result, *bixia* also became a respectful and indirect term of address for the emperor.

No one was allowed to say the emperor's name. It was even forbidden to write it. If, in writing, a character was required that was also used in the emperor's name, the writer was obliged to find another character with a similar meaning. All of these special regulations were known as "taboos to be avoided."

All actions taken by an emperor were described with a unique imperial vocabulary. When an emperor assumed the throne, it was called "ascending to the ultimate." Edicts issued by the emperor were entitled "sacred instructions" or "jade words from the golden mouth." As soon as they were uttered, these carried the force of law. An imperial decree was called an "imperial yellow notice"; written imperial instructions were "comments in vermilion." The imperial residence was called "the palace," "the palace and halls," "the palatial gates," or "the Purple Forbidden City."

An emperor's face was known as his "dragon countenance," and there was a special name for his crown (*mian*). His clothes were known as "dragon robes." When the emperor rode in an imperial cart, the cart was called a "carriage" or "phoenix sedan," and his journeys were called an "imperial progress." The place where he stayed was called a "temporary palace." Places the emperor liked were bestowed with a title that meant good fortune.

The character *yu* was used as a prefix to many things associated with the emperor, such as *yuyong* (things or people employed by the emperor), *yushan* (meals for the emperor), *yulan* (something seen or read by the emperor), *yuzhi* (an imperial edict), *yujia* (royal carriage or movement), *yuyi* (imperial physician), *yulinjun* (imperial guard), and so on. Activities approved by the emperor were prefixed with the character *qin*, such as *qinming* (by imperial order), *qinchai* (imperial envoy), *qinding* (approved by the emperor), and *qinci* (granted by the emperor). The seal used by the emperor was called *xi*, or imperial seal. Even the death of an emperor had its own term, *jiabeng*. The tomb of the emperor was called a *ling*, a royal mound or mausoleum.

At the beginning of the twentieth century, the Forbidden City in Beijing was still an imperial palace, a forbidden and sacred precinct that the ordinary person did not dare approach. From the early years of the Ming dynasty (1368–1644) and the establishment of the Forbidden City in 1421, to the last Qing Emperor, Xuantong (r. 1908–1911), who relinquished his position in 1911, how many tragedies and comedies have been played out here? We can only guess at how much history has taken place in 490 years in this 720,000-square-foot patch of forbidden territory.

Generations of aristocrats and emperors have passed on. But the objects they left behind— the imposing halls, the luxurious furnishings, the rare jewels, the elegant writing implements and daily articles—are still arrayed here today before our eyes. Even the very flagstones of the Forbidden City, worn to concavity by so many shoes, remind us of the comings and goings of innumerable imperial relatives, powerful figures, generals and ministers, as well as eunuchs, palace maidens, artisans, and laborers.

The life of the court, and especially the lives of empresses and concubines of the Qing emperors, has never been addressed in any detail by the documents of the imperial family. As a result, court life has seemed even more mysterious. How were the solemn and magnificent rituals and ceremonies within the palace carried out? How did the emperor, who was busy with myriad duties every day, administer affairs of state? How were the food, drink, and accommodations of the empress managed? Did the emperor engage in cultural activities? What customs and beliefs were followed within the palace? These matters are avidly pursued today by those concerned with Chinese history.

No ceremony was more important than the enthronement, or "ascension to the ultimate." In the early morning on the day of the event, guard soldiers were stationed at all gates of the Forbidden City. Cabinet officials, together with members of the Board of Rites and the highest-ranking officials of the Court of State Ceremonials, set the imperial seal on a table in the Hall of Supreme Harmony (*Taihedian*) directly south of the throne, in a central position.

A table with calligraphed greetings from ministers and officials was placed in the southern part of the eastern section of the hall. The imperial edict was placed directly to its north. Writing brushes and an inkstone were set on a table in the western section, inside the hall proper. A yellow table was put outside the hall in the center of the terrace above the flight of stairs.

Beijing's mysterious Forbidden City was the seat of imperial power for fourteen Ming and ten Qing emperors over a period of 490 years. Construction began in 1406 under the reign of the third Ming emperor, Zhu Di (r. 1402–1424), known as the Yongle emperor, who moved the capital from Nanjing to meet the threat to the empire of the Mongol Yuan dynasty, which had ruled China from 1227 to 1368. The Yongle emperor's tomb, Changling, is the largest in the Ming dynasty funerary park near Beijing and lies at the end of the Sacred Way (*overleaf*).

Officials in charge of the imperial carriage arranged a display of the imperial insignia in front of the hall and through the courtyards. Groups of musicians were posted under the eastern and western eaves of the hall.

From the Meridian Gate (*Wumen*), all the way to the Gate of Heavenly Peace (*Tiananmen*), gigantic imperial insignia and groups of musicians lined both sides of the imperial way. A man with a small dragon pavilion to carry the imperial edict and another with a small pavilion to carry an incense burner stood waiting outside the Meridian Gate. The mood of the event was stately and solemn.

As soon as the new emperor assumed his position in the Hall of Supreme Harmony, three rounds of firecrackers were set off in front of the hall. At the command of the Master of Ceremonies, all ministers and officials performed nine kowtows; they kneeled three times, each time touching their heads against the ground three times. The orchestra played loudly below the stairs. The Grand Secretary read the congratulatory scrolls.

The last part of the ceremony was the proclamation of the imperial edict, signifying that the emperor was the true Son of Heaven, that he accepted the will of heaven, earth, and his ancestors. As the sovereign, he now assumed control of everything under heaven in order to govern the nation, proclaiming his principles of administration and issuing a general amnesty.

Once more, firecrackers were set off; the emperor then returned to his inner palace. All the ministers and officials then parted and moved

through two side gates of the Gate of Supreme Harmony, the Gate that Illuminates Virtue (*Zhaodemen*), and the Gate of Purity Crossing-through (*Zhengdemen*). They followed the imperial edict, which had been placed in the small dragon pavilion, through the Meridian Gate south to the Gate of Heavenly Peace. From the top of the Gate of Heavenly Peace, the edict announcing the start of a new reign was formally proclaimed to the people.

The Palace of Heavenly Purity (*Qianqinggong*), the Hall of Prosperity (*Jiaotaidian*), and the Hall of Earthly Tranquility (*Kunninggong*), known as the Three Rear Palaces (*Housangong*), are located in the center of the inner section of the Forbidden City. The Gate of Earthly Tranquility (*Kunningmen*) is to their north. These buildings form a cluster within the palace and are where the emperor spent much of his time. The buildings are linked by corridors and flanked by six halls to the east and west.

According to records from the early years of his reign, the everyday life of the Qianlong emperor of the Qing Dynasty (r. 1736–1795) was as follows: After getting up in the morning, he would eat a bowl of sweetened bird's nest soup. He would then go either to the western studio in the Palace of Heavenly Purity or to the studio in the Hall of Mental Cultivation (*Yangxindian*) to read a bit of history or some of the classics. He would have breakfast around eight o'clock while surveying the name tablets of the princes and ministers petitioning to see him.

After breakfast, he would read or write instructions on memorials presented to him by

Eighteen facing pairs of carved marble human and animal statues line the Sacred Way, including figures of the mythical *Qilin* (*above*).

Archaeologists have yet to complete the excavation, begun in 1976, of the 8,000 terracotta soldiers, chariots, and horses guarding the tomb of the First Emperor, Qinshihuang.

officials from the capital and the provinces. Then he would receive visiting officials. At around two in the afternoon he would have dinner, and would again read memorials from various ministers and governors submitted by the Grand Secretary. He would eat a light supper in the evening before retiring.

The empress, consorts, and imperial concubines lived in the six halls to the east and west. During the reign of the Kangxi emperor (r. 1662-1722), they numbered fifty-four and held the descending ranks of empress (*hou*), consort (*bin*), imperial concubine (*fei*), worthy lady (*guiren*), palace woman (*changzai*), and responder (*daying*). There was little in the way of a family life in the inner court—the emperor and empress met with their children only on festival days.

Food and clothing are daily necessities for everyone, and emperors are no exception. In the imperial court, unlike among the common people, however, these things were highly politicized. Strict rules were followed, organized around a system of social stratification.

The clothing of the emperor was divided into summer and winter wardrobes, each of which was further divided into clothes to be used on different occasions. There was formal attire for major ceremonies, and there were dragon robes for auspicious days and ordinary garments for ordinary days. There were also clothes for hunting and for rainy weather. In terms of headgear, there were court hats, auspicious hats, daily hats, and hats to be worn on trips. The clothing of the emperor was handled by the Number Four

Storehouse section of the Department of Internal Affairs, whose personnel were always in attendance to assist in changes of clothes.

The emperor's daily meals were provided by the Imperial Kitchen, while those for the empress and imperial concubines were made by kitchens in each palace. Banquets were prepared by the Court of Imperial Entertainments (*Guanglusi*), the Bureau of Provisions in the Ministry of Rites (*Libu jingshan qinglisi*), and the Imperial Kitchen (*Yushanfang*). The grandest were the "Banquets for a Thousand Elders" given during the reigns of the Kangxi and Qianlong emperors. One of these was held in 1796, during the sixty-first year of the reign of the Qianlong emperor, which became the first year of the Jiaqing emperor (r. 1796–1820). After the ceremony, which marked Qianlong's retirement from active government, a "Banquet for a Thousand Elders" was held in the Hall of Ultimate Greatness (*Huangjidian*) in the Palace of Peaceful Longevity (*Ningshougong*). Sitting at eight hundred tables were more than five thousand ministers, officials, soldiers, ordinary people, and craftsmen, every one of whom was over sixty years old. Its splendor was unprecedented.

The cultural life of the Qing court was also rich. The first several emperors of the Qing dynasty were very serious about the study of traditional Chinese culture. According to the Kangxi emperor himself, he already loved to study when he was made emperor at the age of eight. By the time he was seventeen or eighteen, he would get up by the fifth watch, that is, before dawn, in order to read before proceeding to affairs of state. Toward evening he would rest awhile, and then

study some more. Despite extreme fatigue, he would not stop. He asked western missionaries to instruct him in astronomy, geography, mathematics, music, and other subjects.

The Shunzhi emperor (r. 1644–1661) was a very capable calligrapher and painter. The inscribed placard above Qiangqing Palace with the characters "Upright, Just, and Intelligent" was written by him. The Kangxi emperor deeply admired the calligraphy of Mi Fu, Zhao Mengfu, and Dong Qichang, and was particularly influenced by the latter. The Qianlong emperor was a most refined Son of Heaven, excelling at poetry, prose, painting, and calligraphy. He wrote more than 43,000 poems in his lifetime, which approaches the total of all Tang poets combined. If judged only by the sheer number of his poems, no other emperor or poet in history could possibly compare to him.

The Qing court emphasized art collecting. Nothing was overlooked in the various categories, which included calligraphy, painting, rare books, bronzes, ceramics, jade objects, and inkstones. By the beginning of the Qianlong reign, the number of paintings from earlier periods collected by the Internal Affairs Department totaled more than ten thousand.

Opera was also a form of entertainment enjoyed by each Qing emperor. Extended operas were staged for days in a row beginning on New Year's Day or on the birthdays of emperors and empresses. Operas were also performed in the palace or imperial gardens on the first and fifteenth day of each month. Other festivals, such as the Beginning of Spring, Mid-Autumn Festival,

Double Ninth Day, Winter Solstice, and New Year's Eve, were observed by operas related in some way to these occasions. Large theatrical stages were constructed in the rear palaces of the Forbidden City and in the imperial gardens.

The offerings of sacrifices to heaven, to the gods, and to ancestors were the most important rituals for emperors through the ages. It was said, "Sacrifice to Heaven is the most important rite." This protocol was performed on the winter solstice every year. Except for unusual circumstances, the emperor officiated in person. Three days before the ceremony, he would fast within the palace. After undertaking a series of complex preparations, on the day before the Sacrifice to Heaven he would ride in the imperial carriage to the Pavilion for Fasting in the Temple of Heaven and fast there for one more day.

On the day of the sacrifice, accompanied by music, the emperor would visit the Round Altar to receive the gods. He would set out offerings of jade and silk, present the frames for the animal sacrifices, read an invocation to the gods, offer wines three times in a goblet (*jue*), and offer meat, then bid good-bye to the gods and watch the burning of the sacrificial articles. He would also lead all of the assembled officials in the ceremony of repeatedly kowtowing nine times before the ceremony was considered properly completed.

The Imperial Ancestral Temple (*Taimiao*) was the primary site for making sacrifices to ancestors. The emperor was obliged to sacrifice to his ancestors in the temple at the beginning of each of the four seasons. On the occasion of

Chimes, such as the Qianlong era set at Shenyang Palace (*above*), were an important part of court ritual. Audiences with Qing emperors and imperial ceremonies were held in the Great Hall of Administration (*background above*). The palace complex was begun in 1625 by Nurhaci, the northern ruler who united the Qing in the declining years of the Ming dynasty.

birthdays of former emperors, anniversaries of certain deaths, the Qingming Festival in spring, New Year's Eve, and so on, the emperor would go to perform the rites. At the beginning of every month, the emperor would also have to offer greetings to his ancestors. On each occasion, he would first have to fast. Then he would visit the Imperial Ancestral Temple to make offerings. After burning incense, he would kowtow to the departed ancestors.

In the thirty-seventh year of Qianlong (1772), the Qianlong emperor was sixty-two years old and felt that he had become so advanced in age that he might make mistakes in the Triennial Ancestral Sacrifice (*Xiaji*), which would indicate a lack of respect. So, every third year from that year on, he sent eight royal princes, including some of his sons, to burn incense and do the rites for him on the day before New Year's. In 1795, however,

when he was determined at last to step down from his responsibilities as emperor at the venerable age of eighty-five, he went by himself to the Imperial Ancestral Temple. Alone, he burned incense and bowed in reverence to show respect for his ancestors and demonstrate his sincerity.

The deaths of the Qing emperors were treated like those of other emperors and kings through the ages. Each one had an imperial tomb on a grand scale and sacrifices continued to be offered to them during each of the four seasons. Thus, the imperial tombs also became the sites of important sacrifices.

CATALOGUE OF
THE EXHIBITION

By

ZHAO GUSHAN

RESEARCH FELLOW
CHINA CULTURAL RELICS PROMOTION CENTER, BEIJING

Translated by

RICHARD E. STRASSBERG

PROFESSOR OF CHINESE, DEPARTMENT OF EAST ASIAN LANGUAGES AND CULTURES
UNIVERSITY OF CALIFORNIA, LOS ANGELES

Relics from the
Tomb of Marquis Yi of Zeng
from the Warring States Period (475–221 B.C.)

In the summer of 1978, Chinese archaeologists in Hubei province discovered a large tomb at Leigudun in the northwest part of Sui district (the modern city of Suizhou). A great number of bronze vessels were excavated bearing inscriptions such as "Made for Marquis Yi of Zeng" and "Made for the Perpetual Use of Marquis Yi of Zeng," indicating that this was the tomb of a person named "Yi," ruler of the state of Zeng. Among the objects found in the tomb was a bronze bell bearing the seal of Xiongzhang, King Hui of Chu (r. 488–432 B.C.), and a memorial inscription to the ruler of the state of Zeng dated in the year 433 B.C. Thus, the marquis probably died in 433 B.C., more than 2,400 years ago.

Bronze bells from the fifth-century B.C. tomb of Marquis Yi of Zeng, one of the rarest archaeological finds in China.

The tomb of Marquis Yi of Zeng is the type without an entrance passage. It was built as a vertical pit 42.6 feet deep, and measures 42.6 feet from east to west, 54 feet north to south, and 2,300 square feet in area. The coffin was placed at the bottom of the pit and enclosed in a 10-foot high wooden outer coffin consisting of 171 stacked rectangular planks (approximately 13,420 cubic feet of wood). The space around the coffin was filled with more than 66 tons of charcoal beneath 4 to 12 inches of green clay, 8 feet of packed earth, and a top layer of earth. These procedures were designed to deter grave robbers. Charcoal was used to prevent deterioration of the body from water seepage.

The burial vault was divided by wooden walls into four chambers—east, north, west, and central. Each chamber was connected to the others by square tunnels at the base of the walls. The main coffin was placed in the principal chamber on the eastern side of the tomb, and was accompanied by eight additional coffins and the coffin of a sacrificed dog. The western chamber contained thirteen coffins; funerary objects were placed in the central and northern chambers. The principal occupant of the tomb was a male, Yi, who died at approximately forty-five years of age. The accompanying bodies were females ranging in age from thirteen to twenty-five, presumably Yi's wives, concubines, or servant girls.

The tomb of Marquis Yi of Zeng was rich in funerary objects. At the time of his death, Zeng, one of the lesser Warring States, was a major center for bronze working, and the marquis's tomb contained 10 tons of bronze artifacts—the most ever found in a Chinese tomb. Zeng culture, which owed much to the more powerful state of Chu to the south, was rich in other ways as well. A sophisticated material life included highly developed music, splendid cuisine, and extensive use of fragrant plants and flowers in rituals and in daily life. Buried with the marquis were more than 10,000 bronze ritual vessels, objects for daily use and for use with chariots and horses, lacquered wood and bamboo ware, gold and jade objects, texts written on bound bamboo slats, and musical instruments.

Extravagant burials were widespread in ancient China. Death was regarded as similar to life, and all of the things a person might use while alive were moved into his tomb for use in the underworld. Because of this belief, a ruler's wife, concubines, and servant girls were ritually sacrificed to accompany him in burial, a custom that continued unbroken through the Spring and Autumn period (770–475 B.C.) and ended by the time of the Han dynasty (206 B.C.–A.D. 220).

Altogether, 134 bronze vessels of 38 different types were excavated from the tomb of Marquis Yi of Zeng. Most were found in their original places in the central chamber and reflect the way the occupant used them during his life. The northern chamber contained more than 4,500 bronze weapons, including daggers, halberds, spears, bows, arrows, shields, and armor.

Marquis Yi's tomb was well sealed and never robbed and also preserved many lacquered wood, gold, and jade objects, as well as 125 musical instruments made of wood and bronze. The

A scale model of the tomb of Marquis Yi of Zeng. Discovered in 1978, the tomb yielded more than 10,000 bronze vessels.

instruments were arranged in the central chamber and included a set of bells (*bianzhong*), a set of chimes (*bianqing*), drums (*gu*), pitch pipes (*paixiao*), flutes (*hu*), mouth organs (*sheng*), and two kinds of zithers (*qin* and *se*). Many of these instruments—the set of pitch pipes, the flute and bronze drum, the ten- and five-stringed zithers—had never before been seen.

The set of bronze bells, 65 in all with a combined weight of 5,500 pounds, was one of the rarest finds in all of Chinese archaeology. Inscriptions engraved on the bells—more than 3,700 ideographs, most of which are cast in gold—can be divided into those that define tonal pitches and those that present standard pitches. The standard-pitch inscriptions set forth the names of the standard pitches, scales, and altered pitches used in feudal states such as Chu, Jin, Qi, Zhou, and Shen and the relationships between them. Of the 53 inscriptions about standard pitches, 35 were previously unknown. When compared with present-day measurements, it was discovered that the tones were accurate. Each bell can produce a tone that spans three steps of the scale, and the entire range extends more than five octaves; the middle octave contains a complete range of 12 half-tones. Moreover, the set of bells is capable of modulating pitch and key. Even today, many musical pieces can still be performed on it.

**BRONZE *HUODING* WITH
PAIR OF HOOKS AND SPOON**

Height 64.6 cm (25.2 in)
Diameter of mouth 64.2 cm (25 in)
Height of feet 33.6 cm (13.1 in)
Weight 54.8 kg (121 lb)

Length of hooks 24.8 cm (9.7 in)
Length of spoon 158.5 cm (62 in)

Excavated in 1978 from the tomb
of Marquis Yi of Zeng in Sui district, Hubei

Hubei Provincial Museum

The *huoding* is a vessel for food used in important
rituals. This example is elaborately decorated with
patterns of hanging leaves, interlaced serpents,
and geometric clouds. Dragons are carved in relief
on the upper legs, and in the middle is a pattern
of protruding shapes. Inside on the bottom is an
inscription, "Made for the Perpetual Use of
Marquis Yi of Zeng," written in two columns of
seven ideographs. When excavated, it still
contained a piece of ox bone, and the underside
preserved traces of fire. The hooks were attached

to the loops of the vessel, and the spoon was found
placed against the rim. The hooks and spoon were
cast with inscriptions similar to that on the *huoding*.

According to Zheng Xuan's (A.D.
127–200) commentary on the *Book of Ritual* (*Liji*),
a Confucian classic presenting proper ritual
ceremonies of Zhou dynasty China, "The *huo* is a
vessel used to boil meat, fish, and dried meat,"
indicating that the *huoding* was used by the nobility
to cook meat during sacrifices and at banquets.
The *huo* was a large cooking vessel. The *ding*, a
tripod vessel used for cooking meat, eventually
came to symbolize rank; the more *ding* present in a
tomb, the higher the occupant's rank. The
expression "hacked and sawed into pieces and
cooked in a *huoding*" refers to a cruel method of
execution in ancient times.

This *huo* is derived from the giant *huo*
vessel of the Central Plains, but its narrow neck
and slanted shoulders reflect a style unique to Chu
culture, demonstrating the influence upon Zeng
of the more powerful Chu kingdom to the south.

BRONZE *SHENGDING*
WITH SPOON

Height 35.5 cm (13.8 in)
Diameter of mouth 45.8 cm (17.9 in)
Diameter of body 38.4 cm (15 in)
Weight 20.6 kg (45.5 lb)
Length of spoon 45.8 cm (17.9 in)

Excavated in 1978 from the tomb
of Marquis Yi of Zeng in
Sui district, Hubei

Hubei Provincial Museum

The *shengding* was another vessel for food used in important rituals. A pattern of dragons with bird heads was originally inlaid in turquoise on the body of the vessel, but the turquoise had fallen out by the time of excavation. The outer walls contain a secondary decoration of four dragons. Swirling clouds are carved in relief on the upper portion of the feet; in the middle is a pattern of protruding shapes.

This *shengding* is one of a matching set. When the spoon was excavated, it was found placed inside one of the vessels. The handle of the spoon is incised with a geometric openwork pattern. Inscribed on the inside wall of the vessel and on the spoon handle is, "Made for the Perpetual Use of Marquis Yi of Zeng."

Studies of the uses of *ding* vessels during the Zhou dynasty reveal that each type of *ding* had a different function. According to Zheng Xuan's commentary on the *Book of Etiquette and Ceremonial* (*Ili*), another well-known Confucian classic of ritual literature, cooking in a *huoding* was called

"*peng*," while meat cooked in a *ding* vessel was called "*sheng*." In sacrificial rituals, the meat was first cooked in *huoding*, while *shengding* were the main vessels used when it was offered up. Thus, the *shengding* was considered by the ancients as "the most formal *ding* vessel." The number of such vessels at a sacrifice was an indication of status.

BRONZE *GUI*

Height 31.8 cm (12.4 in)
Diameter of mouth 22.2 cm (8.7 in)
Length of base 23.2 cm (9 in)
Width 23 cm (8.9 in)
Weight 12.8 kg (28 lb)

Excavated in 1978 from the tomb
of Marquis Yi of Zeng in Sui district, Hubei

Hubei Provincial Museum

BRONZE COVERED *DING*
WITH OX-SHAPED KNOB
AND TWO HOOKS

Height 39.3 cm (15.3 in)
Diameter of mouth 39.6 cm (15.4 in)
Weight 25.3 kg (55.9 lb)

Excavated in 1978 from the tomb
of Marquis Yi of Zeng in Sui district, Hubei

Hubei Provincial Museum

During the Zhou dynasty, *huoding* and *shengding* were the main vessels used in the ritual preparation of food, but there were also subsidiary vessels called "*xiuding*." This *ding* is one of the subsidiary vessels found in the tomb of Marquis Yi. The cover is decorated with three knobs in the lively and realistic shape of an ox. On their bodies are patterns of swirling clouds and animal masks. The cover and outer walls were inlaid with turquoise patterns, but most of the turquoise had fallen out by the time of excavation. The most prevalent pattern is that of a coiled dragon interlaced with clouds. The inscriptions inside the cover and on the inside wall read, "Made for the Perpetual Use of Marquis Yi of Zeng." When excavated, the vessel still contained an ox bone, and the exterior bore traces of fire.

The *gui* (*facing page*) is a traditional form of vessel characteristic of the Zhou culture of the Central Plains region, and was also used to prepare food in important rituals. On the square base and in the center of the cover are buttons in the shape of a five-petaled lotus flower. Attached to both sides of the body are dragon-shaped loops. The vessel is covered with linked patterns of clouds, interlaced phoenixes, linked outlines, lozenge patterns, and patterns of dragons with bird heads, all inlaid in turquoise. In certain portions, a small amount of turquoise remains in the grooves of the inlay. Eight such vessels, known as the "eight *gui*," were recovered from the tomb. In the regulations for rituals during the Zhou dynasty, an odd number of *ding* vessels were to be employed with an even number of *gui* at sacrifices and banquets. The *ding* were filled with meat, and the *gui* with millet or other grains. Heads of state were buried with eight *gui* and nine *ding*, the number of each found with Marquis Yi.

BRONZE *PAN* TRAY WITH
ZUN WINE CONTAINER

Height of *zun* 30.1 cm (11.7 in)
Width of mouth 25 cm (9.8 in)
Weight 9 kg (20 lb)

Height of *pan* 23.5 cm (9.2 in)
Width of mouth 58 cm (23 in)
Weight 19.2 kg (42.4 lb)

Excavated in 1978 from the tomb
of Marquis Yi of Zeng in Sui district, Hubei

Hubei Provincial Museum

This is a wine vessel composed of a *zun* container and a *pan* tray. The *zun* was filled with wine and the *pan* held water. According to the *Book of Ritual*, "A tray holding ice is used at important funerals." Thus, a *pan* could also hold ice at important rituals such as sacrifices. When excavated, the *zun* was found placed in the *pan*, indicating that it was used for cooling wine. This elaborate vessel was manufactured with delicacy and care, making it a famous example of a rare bronze from ancient China. Its most striking aspect is the pierced design of a stylized serpent along the mouths of both pieces. Also of particular note is the intricacy of the openwork decoration of a dragon around the neck of the *zun*.

Research reveals that the *zun* was constructed of 34 separate pieces and the *pan* of 38 pieces. The parts were joined by casting or welding, and the bodies of the *zun* and *pan* were cast from molds. Scientific analysis has determined that the pierced decoration used a complex technique known today as "section-mold assembly." The outer surface of bronze seams creates delicate and beautiful designs, while the inner surface serves as structural support. The

inner layer of bronze also indicates an ingenious use of the lost-wax process of the section-mold assembly method. In the history of metal-casting in China, this *zun* and *pan*—one of the earliest known examples of its kind—demonstrates that as early as the pre-Qin period (before 221 B.C.), China had already mastered the technique of section-mold assembly.

LARGE BRONZE *ZUNFOU*

Height 126 cm (49 in)
Diameter of mouth 48.2 (19 in)
Diameter of body 100 cm (39 in)

Diameter of base 70.4 cm (27 in)
Weight 327.5 kg (724 lb)

Excavated in 1978 from the tomb
of Marquis Yi of Zeng in
Sui district, Hubei

Hubei Provincial Museum

The *zunfou* was used to store wine. The body of the vessel was cast in two parts, which were then joined. Along the shoulder is inscribed in two lines of seven characters each, "Made for the Perpetual Use of Marquis Yi of Zeng." On the cover are four rings facing each other, and on the side of the cover is another ring attached to a chain formed by two links and a pair of rings. One end is connected to a ring in the shape of a snake on the shoulder of the vessel, so that the cover is not completely detached from the vessel when opened. Around the middle of the body, encircled above and below by protruding belts, are four equally spaced rings used to lift the vessel.

Two examples of this kind of *zunfou* were excavated from the tomb of Marquis Yi. They are the largest wine vessels yet found dating from the Zhou dynasty.

GUANFOU INLAID WITH COPPER

Height 35.9 cm (14 in)
Diameter of body 43.5 cm (17 in)
Weight 36.5 kg (80.6 lb)

Excavated in 1978 from the tomb
of Marquis Yi of Zeng in Sui district, Hubei

Hubei Provincial Museum

This is a vessel for water used in important rituals. In the center of the cover is a handle in the shape of a trumpet. On the body are two ring holders in the shape of animal masks. Attached to the ring holders are three-link chains used to lift the vessel. Covering most of the surface are designs in copper created by the cast-inlay technique. The most prevalent of these are linked clouds, lozenge shapes, coiled dragons, dragons with bird heads, and swirling patterns. Written in seven ideographs inside the cover and on the shoulder of the vessel is the inscription, "Made for the Perpetual Use of Marquis Yi of Zeng."

In the rituals of the Zhou dynasty, a washing ceremony was performed at sacrifices and banquets. The *guanfou* was filled with water, which was then poured out for washing and caught in a basin (*pan*).

IMPERIAL
TOMBS
OF CHINA
中国皇陵

A *hu* is a wine container and a *jin* is used in ritual ceremonies to display wine vessels. Very few bronze *jin* have been excavated. Only four have been discovered up until now, and this is the only example of a set of *hu* together with a *jin*. The surface of the *jin* is rectangular with four feet in the shape of animals. The mouth and front limbs of the animals grasp the surface of the *jin*, while the rear feet provide support. The surface of the *jin* has two round depressions for holding the circular feet of the large *hu*. This *jin* together with the *hu* clearly comprise a matched set, something found infrequently in ancient China. One of the important features of the tomb of Marquis Yi is the large number of sets of vessels found in the burial. The size and shape of the two

hu are similar. The covers are decorated with an outlined, linked pattern of "T" shapes forming an openwork design. On the top of each cover is a button in the shape of a snake holding a ring. Along both sides of the neck are bent loops in the shape of dragons. On the heads of the dragons are engraved two smaller dragons inside circles, and each of the tails is decorated with yet another small dragon. A ring hangs from each of the dragon-shaped loops. On the body of each vessel are two lozenge-shaped horizontal belts in relief and four vertical belts dividing the body of the *hu* into eight sections. The body is also decorated with a coiled serpent pattern. On the wall of the necks is the inscription, "Made for the Perpetual Use of Marquis Yi of Zeng."

LARGE BRONZE *HU* WITH *JIN*

Height 99 cm (38.6 in)
Diameter of body 53.2 cm (20.7 in)
Weight 240 kg (530 lb)

Excavated in 1978 from the tomb of Marquis Yi of Zeng in Sui district, Hubei

Hubei Provincial Museum

BRONZE *YAN*

Height 64.9 cm (25.3 in)
Diameter of mouth 47.8 cm (18.6 in)
Weight 33.4 kg (73.8 lb)

Excavated in 1978 from the tomb
of Marquis Yi of Zeng in Sui district, Hubei

Hubei Provincial Museum

This is a set of vessels for food composed of a
zeng and a *li*. There are eight holes in the bottom
of the *zeng*. When used, the *li* was filled with
water and the *zeng* with food, which was then
steamed or boiled. The body of the *zeng* is inlaid
with various designs, the principal ones being a
linked pattern of clouds and a pattern of leaves
hanging downward.

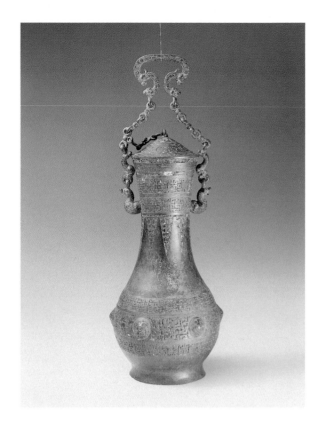

BRONZE *HU* WITH CHAIN

Height 40.5 cm (15.8 in)
Width of mouth 18.9 cm (7.4 in)
Weight 5.6 kg (12.4 lb)

Excavated in 1978 from the tomb
of Marquis Yi of Zeng in Sui district, Hubei

Hubei Provincial Museum

This is a wine vessel. The chain is attached to
loops in the shape of animals and the handle bar
is in the shape of a dragon. The cover is
connected to this chain by another chain. The
hu is decorated with inlays in complex patterns,
the principal ones being plantain leaves and
clouds, swirling patterns, linked clouds, and
shapes like a weaver's shuttle. The manufacture is
exquisite, as evidenced by the intricate designs on
the surfaces of both the handle bar and the chain,
reflecting the characteristic splendor of the Chu
culture. On the wall of the *hu* is inscribed, "Made
for the Perpetual Use of Marquis Yi of Zeng."

TWO SMALL BRONZE *LI* WITH SPOON

Height 12.9 cm (5 in)
Diameter of mouth 15.25 cm (5.9 in)
Length of spoon 18.5 cm (7.2 in)

Excavated in 1978 from the tomb
of Marquis Yi of Zeng in Sui district, Hubei

Hubei Provincial Museum

The *li* was also a vessel for food. The bodies of these *li* are inlaid with a pattern of bird heads and clouds. Along the edge of the mouth is the inscription in seven ideographs, "Made for the Perpetual Use of Marquis Yi of Zeng." When it was excavated, the spoon was found placed in one of the *li* and bears the same inscription.

TWO BRONZE VESSELS IN THE SHAPE
OF A *DING* WITH TWO SPOONS

Height 20.7 cm (8.1 in)
Width of mouth 11.8 cm (4.6 in)
Length of spoons 18.7 cm (7.3 in)

Excavated in 1978 from the tomb
of Marquis Yi of Zeng in Sui district, Hubei

Hubei Provincial Museum

The bodies of these bronze vessels in the shape of
a *ding* are inlaid with designs in turquoise, the
principal ones being linked clouds and leaves
hanging downward. When excavated, each vessel
contained a spoon.

SHALLOW BRONZE *DOU*

Height 21.6 cm (8.4 in)
Diameter of mouth 21.4 cm (8.3 in)
Weight 4.2 kg (9 lb)

Excavated in 1978 from the tomb
of Marquis Yi of Zeng in Sui district, Hubei

Hubei Provincial Museum

Also used for food, this vessel is decorated with
patterns of inlaid turquoise, the most important of
which are linked dragons and phoenixes, linked
clouds, and leaves hanging downward. Inside the
pan is the inscription, "Made for the Perpetual Use
of Marquis Yi of Zeng." According to the *Book of
Ritual*, a *dou* is a vessel especially used to hold food
such as salted vegetables and mashed meat cooked
with soybean sauce. The text stipulated that "in the
ritual ceremonies of the nobility, dukes are
permitted forty *dou*, marquis and earls, thirty-two,
viscounts and barons, twenty-four." Other literary
sources indicate that there was a custom among the
common people that "those who attain sixty years
of age are served food in three *dou*, those who
attain seventy years, in four *dou*, eighty years, in five
dou, and ninety years, in six *dou*" to demonstrate
respect for the elderly.

PAIR OF BRONZE WEIGHTS
WITH DRAGON DESIGN

Height 8 cm (3.1 in)
Length 11.8 cm (4.6 in)

Excavated in 1978 from the tomb
of Marquis Yi of Zeng in Sui district, Hubei

Hubei Provincial Museum

The people of the Warring States period sat on
bamboo mats, and weights such as these were used
to prevent the edges of the mats from curling. On
top of each is a knob in the shape of a dragon
with a ring for lifting. The surfaces are cast with
eight intertwined dragons, their bodies decorated
with a pattern of scales. Between the dragons are
fourteen circles originally inlaid with decorative
objects that have since fallen out.

Bronze weights were used for practical
purposes, but jade was also common. The section
invoking the Great Emperor of the East in the
"Nine Songs" of the *Songs of Chu* anthology (*Chuci*:
"Jiuge," ca. third century B.C.) states, "Jade weights
are placed on the jasper mats." Wang Yi's (ca. A.D.
89–158) commentary on this text also notes that
"weights of white jade were used to fix the mats."

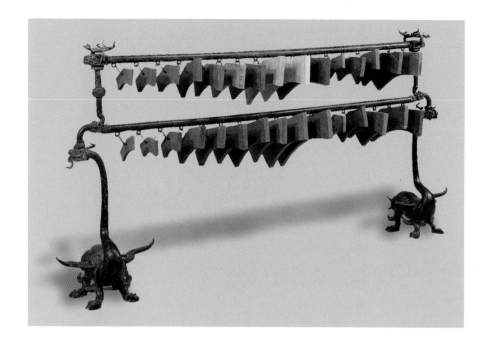

SET OF CHIMES
WITH BRONZE FRAME
(*BIANQING*)

Height 109 cm (42.5 in)
Length 215 cm (83.9 in)

Excavated in 1978 from
the tomb of Marquis Yi of
Zeng in Sui district, Hubei

Hubei Provincial Museum

During the Zhou dynasty, there were strict regulations concerning the use of chimes, an ancient Chinese percussion instrument. Only aristocrats were permitted to employ them, and their size was based on rank. Most of the chimes in this set were damaged, but the rack is well preserved. It is constructed of a pair of standing supports and two horizontal beams. Each support consists of a cylindrical bronze pillar on top of a base in the shape of a strange animal. These strange animals are a composite of a dragon head, crane neck, bird body, and turtle feet. The necks of both animals turn outward as though singing. Their eyes protrude and their long tongues spiral downward. On the tongues is the inscription, "Made for the Perpetual Use of Marquis Yi of Zeng."

Attached to the lower of the two horizontal beams are seventeen bronze rings from which the chimes are hung. There are dragon heads at the points where the vertical supports and the horizontal beams meet. In addition to the pairs of wings and four feet, the entire bronze rack is decorated with cloud and swirling patterns cast in gold. The lines of the inlay are slender and dense, forming a tightly organized design.

This set of chimes with rack displays complexity of craftsmanship, a beautiful form, and a unique conception. It reflects the aesthetics and religious concepts of the ancient Chinese and is a rare treasure.

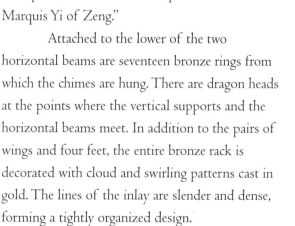

BRONZE COVERED *DOU*
WITH TURQUOISE INLAY

Height 26.4 cm (10.3 in)
Diameter of mouth 20.6 cm (8 in)
Weight 5.9 kg (13 lb)

Excavated in 1978 from the tomb
of Marquis Yi of Zeng in Sui district, Hubei

Hubei Provincial Museum

This food vessel is decorated in exquisite patterns of inlaid turquoise. In the center of the cover is a design of interlaced phoenixes, and the outer ring contains four groups of dragons with bird heads. On the body are paired facing patterns of bird heads and clouds. The stem and base have patterns of stylized coiled dragons. The inside of the cover and the inner wall of the vessel bear the inscription, "Made for the Perpetual Use of Marquis Yi of Zeng."

The entire vessel is well preserved and a rare example of its kind.

BRONZE HEATING *PAN*

Height 14 cm (5.5 in)
Diameter of mouth 43.8 cm (17 in)
Weight 16.2 kg (35.8 lb)

Excavated in 1978 from the tomb
of Marquis Yi of Zeng in Sui district, Hubei

Hubei Provincial Museum

This is a practical object used for heating. It has a pair of side rings attached to double chains, and rests on three feet in the shape of animals. The body of the vessel bears a design in copper created by the cast-inlay technique. The most prevalent patterns are composed of shapes like a weaver's shuttle and linked clouds. When excavated, a bronze winnower and a shovel pierced with holes were found placed inside, as shown below. On the underside of the vessel in the center is the inscription, "Made for the Perpetual Use of Marquis Yi of Zeng."

BRONZE WINNOWER (*JI*)

Height 5.2 cm (2 in)
Length 29 cm (11.3 in)
Diameter of mouth 25.3 cm (9.8 in)

Excavated in 1978 from the tomb
of Marquis Yi of Zeng
in Sui district, Hubei

Hubei Provincial Museum

The pattern on this bronze winnower imitates
woven bamboo. Along the edge of the mouth is
the inscription, "Made for the Perpetual Use of
Marquis Yi of Zeng." When excavated, it was
found placed in the heating *pan* (*opposite*).

BRONZE PIERCED SHOVEL (*LOUCHAN*)

Length 38.6 cm (15 in)
Width at the mouth 14.7 cm (5.7 in)

Excavated in 1978 from the tomb
of Marquis Yi of Zeng in Sui district, Hubei

Hubei Provincial Museum

The curved edges and outer wall of this shovel
bear a design in copper from the cast-inlay
technique. The most prevalent patterns are
formed by coiled dragons and roughly executed
clouds. On the handle is the inscription, "Made
for the Perpetual Use of Marquis Yi of Zeng."
When excavated, it was found inside the heating
pan (*opposite*).

GOLD BOWL AND SPOON

Bowl: height 11 cm (4.3 in)
Diameter of mouth 15.1 cm (5.8 in)
Weight 2150 g (75.9 oz)

Spoon: length 13 cm (5 in); weight 50 g (1.8 oz)

Excavated in 1978 from the tomb
of Marquis Yi of Zeng in Sui district, Hubei

Hubei Provincial Museum

This gold bowl and spoon were buried in the inner coffin with the Marquis Yi of Zeng. The spoon had been placed in the bowl, indicating that the two were employed as a set. The bowl was used to hold food, and the pierced spoon was used to stir and scoop food from broth. This bowl and spoon, which display skillful workmanship and are 98% pure, are the heaviest gold objects to have been excavated so far in China. The high

degree of accomplishment demonstrated in these objects indicates the importance of craftsmanship in gold during the pre-Qin period.

COVERED *DOU* IN CARVED WOOD
WITH COLORED LACQUER

Height 24.3 cm (9.5 in)

Excavated in 1978 from the tomb
of Marquis Yi of Zeng in Sui district, Hubei

Hubei Provincial Museum

This is a food vessel consisting of a cover and a *dou* with side handles. The cup is oval-shaped and on both sides are high, square handles carved in relief. On both sides of the oval-shaped cover are holes in the shape of a crescent moon intended for inlay. On the top of the cover are three intertwined dragons carved in relief. The two carved handles form animal masks also composed of dragons carved in relief. The scales on the bodies of these dragons are intricately engraved. The vessel is covered with a black lacquer background on which elaborate patterns are painted in red and yellow lacquer. Some designs are painted on intaglio carving. The most prevalent of these patterns are clouds, caltrops, linked patterns, stylized phoenixes, and phoenixes. This covered *dou* is well preserved and illustrates the high level of ancient Chinese lacquer craft.

CLOTHING BOX WITH PAINTED DESIGN OF THE TWENTY-EIGHT CONSTELLATIONS

Length 82.8 cm (32.3 in)
Height 40.5 cm (15.8 in)
Width 47 cm (18.3 in)

Excavated in 1978 from the tomb
of Marquis Yi of Zeng in Sui district, Hubei

Hubei Provincial Museum

The cover and body of this box are constructed of two separate pieces of hollowed-out wood. The cover fits over a tenon on the body. Protruding from the top of the vaulted cover on both sides are convex-shaped feet used when the top is removed and stored. On the box is an inscription identifying it as a clothing trunk. The inside is coated with black and vermilion lacquer; on the outside is a black lacquer ground. Written in seal-style script in the center of the top is the large ideograph "*Dou*" (斗), "Dipper." The names of the twenty-eight constellations are written in a circle surrounding "*Dou*" according to their proper astronomical order. "The third day of the month *jiayin*" is written beneath the ideograph for the constellation "*Kang*" (堅). At each end of the cover, the Green Dragon of the east and the White Tiger of the west are painted in red lacquer. Opposite the Green Dragon is a large mushroom-shaped cloud, as well as two crosses like the ideograph "*shi*" (十), "ten," and a pattern of dots. The mythical toad who dwells in the moon is painted opposite the White Tiger. Painted on one side of the container are two animals facing each other; painted along the other side is a red belt.

TWO JADE RINGS (*JUE*) WITH CLOUD PATTERN

First ring: diameter 5 cm (1.9 in)
Diameter of hole 2.4–2.6 cm (0.9–1 in)

Second ring: diameter 5.2 cm (2 in)
Diameter of hole 2.4 cm (0.9 in)

Excavated in 1978 from the tomb of Marquis Yi of Zeng
in Sui district, Hubei

Hubei Provincial Museum

Both sides of these decorative objects are engraved with cloud patterns. Rings such as these are among the type of jade ornaments worn hanging from the belt. However, they have a special significance reflected in the phrase, "When a Noble Man makes a decision [*jue*], he breaks the jade ring [*jue*] hanging from his belt," recorded in Duan Yucai's (A.D. 1735–1815) commentary on the dictionary *Explanations of Ideographs* (*Shuowen jiezi*, early second century A.D.), in which he cites the *White Tiger Hall Discussions* (*Baihutong*, first century A.D.).

In "Basic Annals of Xiang Yu" in the *Historical Records* (*Shiji*: "Xiang Yu benzhuan"), at the banquet at Hongmen, Xiang Yu (233–202 B.C.), the Hegemon-King of Western Chu, could not decide whether to kill his rival, Liu Bang (256–195 B.C.), later the first emperor of the Han dynasty. "Fan Zeng [Xiang Yu's advisor] stared at him several times and thrice lifted the jade ring from his belt as a sign," thus employing the meaning of the jade ring as "decide." *Jue* can also mean "breaking relations," as in the song lamenting the Goddess of the Xiang River in the "Nine Songs" of the *Songs of Chu* anthology (*Chuci*: "Jiuge") where the poet Qu Yuan (ca. 340–278 B.C.) states, "I cast my jade ring into the Yangtze." At that time, when a ruler bestowed a closed circular ring (*huan*) on an official, it signified "retirement" (*guihuan*). When he bestowed a *jue*, it signified "break" and meant exile. When Qu Yuan cast his ring into the river, he was expressing the wish that the King of Chu might recall him to the court so that he could serve the state.

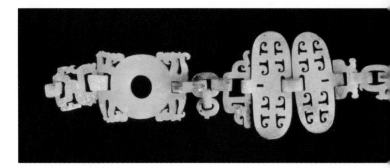

SEMICIRCULAR JADE (*HUANG*) JOINED WITH GOLD WIRE

Length 11.8 cm (4.6 in); width 2.7 cm (1 in)

Excavated in 1978 from the tomb of
Marquis Yi of Zeng in Sui district, Hubei

Hubei Provincial Museum

Three gold wires join two unequal pieces of jade
to form a rare decorative object. Cloud patterns
are carved onto both sides.

SEMICIRCULAR JADE WITH PIERCED DRAGON DESIGN

Length 15.2 cm (6 in); width 4.6 cm (2 in)

Excavated in 1978 from the tomb of
Marquis Yi of Zeng in Sui district, Hubei

Hubei Provincial Museum

This rare decorative object from the Warring
States period is exquisitely carved in a pierced
design of four dragons and six snakes.

DRAGON AND PHOENIX JADE BELT IN SIXTEEN SECTIONS (*above*)

Length 48 cm (18.7 in); width 8.3 cm (3.2 in)

Excavated in 1978 from the tomb of
Marquis Yi of Zeng in Sui district, Hubei

Hubei Provincial Museum

This decorative object was found across the
lower jaw of the marquis, leading some to
hypothesize that it was originally a hat
decoration. The belt is composed of sixteen
sections. The first section is in the shape of a
dragon head, and the remaining fifteen sections
form the dragon's body. Each section is carved
either with a dragon and phoenix motif or in the
shape of a ring. Details of the dragon and
phoenix such as mouth, eyes, horns, scales,
feathers, tails, and claws are engraved on both
sides, as are patterns of grain, clouds, and
oblique lines on the rings. In addition to the
overall pierced dragon and phoenix design, other
designs of dragons, phoenixes, and snakes are
carved or engraved on both sides. Altogether
there are thirty-eight dragons, seven phoenixes,
and ten snakes matching on both sides.

Research shows that the belt is made
from five separate pieces of jade which were
divided and then joined into a chain with plain
oval rings and a fastener. Although intricate and
delicate, it can be freely rolled. This beautiful jade
belt combines in a single object the techniques of
carving a single piece into individual linked pieces,
pierced carving, and engraving.

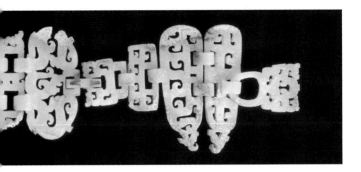

JADE BELT ORNAMENT (*PEI*) OF DRAGONS AND PHOENIXES IN FOUR SECTIONS (*below*)

Length 9.5 cm (3.7 in), width 7.2 cm (2.8 in)

Excavated in 1978 from the tomb of
Marquis Yi of Zeng in Sui district, Hubei

Hubei Provincial Museum

This decorative object is composed of four freely
moving pieces carved from a single piece of jade.
The entire piece contains seven writhing dragons,
four phoenixes, and four snakes. The composition
displays considerable formal beauty. The lines of
the patterns are as delicate as silk threads, making
this a consummate example of Chinese jade
carving during the Warring States period.

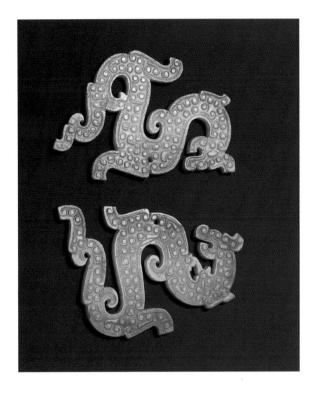

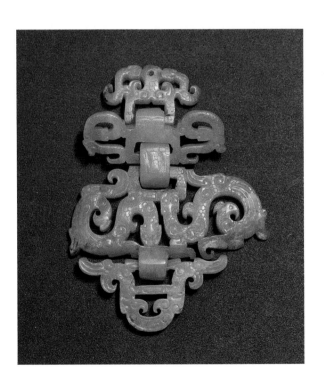

PAIR OF JADE BELT ORNAMENTS IN THE SHAPE OF WRITHING DRAGONS

First dragon:
Length 11.5 cm (4.5 in)
Width 8 cm (3.1 in)

Second dragon:
Length 11.3 cm (4.4 in)
Width 7.7 cm (3 in)

Excavated in 1978 from the tomb
of Marquis Yi of Zeng in Sui district, Hubei

Hubei Provincial Museum

This pair of jade dragons with backward-facing
heads and curving bodies was designed as an
ornament to be worn hanging from the belt. A
grain pattern is carved on the dragons' bodies.

Relics from the
Tomb of the King of Zhongshan
from the Warring States Period (475–221 B.C.)

According to the *Origin of Hereditary Families* (*Shiben*, Han dynasty), the capital of the state of Zhongshan (414–296 B.C.) during its latter period was a city called Lingshou, where five generations of Zhongshan rulers reigned. The territory of the Zhongshan state (not to be confused with the later Western Han kingdom of the same name) extended north to modern Anxin and Xushui in Hebei, south to the southern part of Gaoyi, west to the Taihang Mountains, and east to the Li, Anping, Shen, Xinhe, and Julu districts.

According to another important source, "Hereditary Clan of Zhao" in the *Historical Records* (*Shiji*: "Zhao shijia"), the last Zhongshan king, Shang, was defeated in the third year of the reign of King Huiwen of Zhao (296 B.C.) by an alliance of Zhao with Qi and Yan. King Shang was captured and sent back to his hometown of Fushi (modern Yan'an, Shaanxi), and the state of Zhongshan ceased to exist from then on.

Where exactly was the capital of Lingshou? In 1974, a large, shiny stone was shown to archaeologists working near Sanji township in the southern part of Pingshan district, Hebei. It had been discovered in a stream bed and taken home decades earlier by a local farmer. The water-worn 2 ½-by-3-foot stone bore the two-line inscription, "Royal fishpond watcher Gongcheng

Discovered in 1974 in Pingshan district, Hebei, and excavated from 1974 to 1978, the Bronze Age tombs of the kings of Zhongshan reopened the lost history of the Warring States period Kingdom of Zhongshan (414–296 B.C.) and its ancient capital, Lingshou. The tomb of King Cuo (r. 320–308 B.C.), the third ruler of Zhongshan, was the largest and most elaborate.

IMPERIAL
TOMBS
OF CHINA
中国皇陵

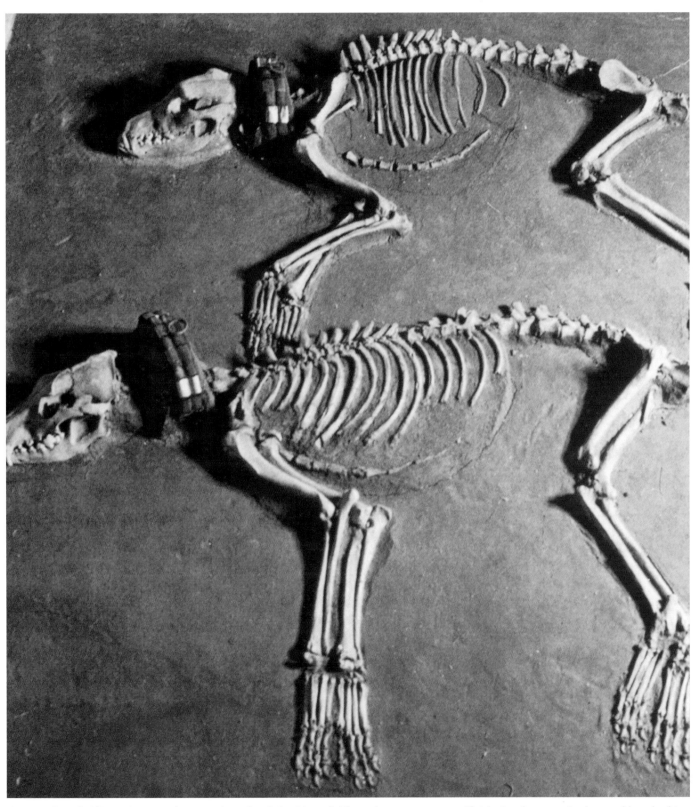

Among the subsidiary pits near the central tomb of the king of Zhongshan were two sacrificial pits that contained everything the king might need for hunting. Found with these objects were the skeletal remains of two large hunting dogs adorned with silver and gold collars.

De and tomb overseer Juijiang Man respectfully greet gentlemen of future generations," clearly indicating that the tombs of the Zhongshan kings were nearby.

Sanji township is located approximately 46.5 miles west of the city of Shijiazhuang in Hebei, along the northern bank of the Hutuo River where the land is hilly. From 1974 to 1978, twenty tombs, two structures above the tombs, two pits of horses and chariots, one sacrificial pit with miscellaneous objects, and a pit with a funerary boat—all from the Spring and Autumn and Warring States periods—were excavated in the region. More than 19,000 objects were collected.

In the eastern part of Sanji township are the ruins of a Warring States city wall (FIG. I-A). It extends 2.5 miles from north to south and more than a mile east to west. Within the walls are the ruins of many houses, as well as places for manufacturing pottery, bronze, and iron objects. All of the tombs that have thus far been excavated have floor plans in the shape of the ideograph "*zhong*" (中), "center." There are three major tombs along a south-to-north axis in the northeastern section of the city (FIG. I-B). West of the southernmost tomb (FIG. I-T6) are three middle-sized tombs (FIGS. I-T3, I-T4, and I-T5) arranged on an east-

Although looted after the kingdom's fall in 296 B.C., the Zhongshan tombs still held a wealth of historical information. Among the objects discovered in the tomb were many bronze vessels and weapons, and more than 350 jade objects.

west axis relative to T6. In the vicinity of these four tombs are sacrificial pits of horses and chariots. All except T5 have pits for accompanying burials. These discoveries showed that T6 is the principal tomb in this cluster, which has been attributed to the second Zhongshan ruler, Duke Cheng (r. ca. 340–320 B.C.), and that these ruins of a city wall from the Warring States period are those of Lingshou, the last capital of Zhongshan.

A number of other tombs from the same period are scattered in locations within a mile and a half west of Lingshou. In particular, two large tombs, TI and T2 (Fig. I), are situated along an east-west axis west of the village of Central Qiji, 1.5 miles west of the city wall of Lingshou. The largest, TI (FIG. 2), is now known to be the tomb of the third Zhongshan ruler, King Cuo (r. ca. 320–308 B.C.); T2 is thought to be the tomb of the royal consort. The king's tomb was built of layers of packed earth and timber in the shape of a square, and was approached by ramps from the north and south. The mound over the tomb was originally surmounted by a shrine and surrounded by galleries, giving it the appearance of a three-level pyramidal structure. The tomb's present height is 49 feet. It measures 300 feet from east to west and 360 feet from north to south. There is a

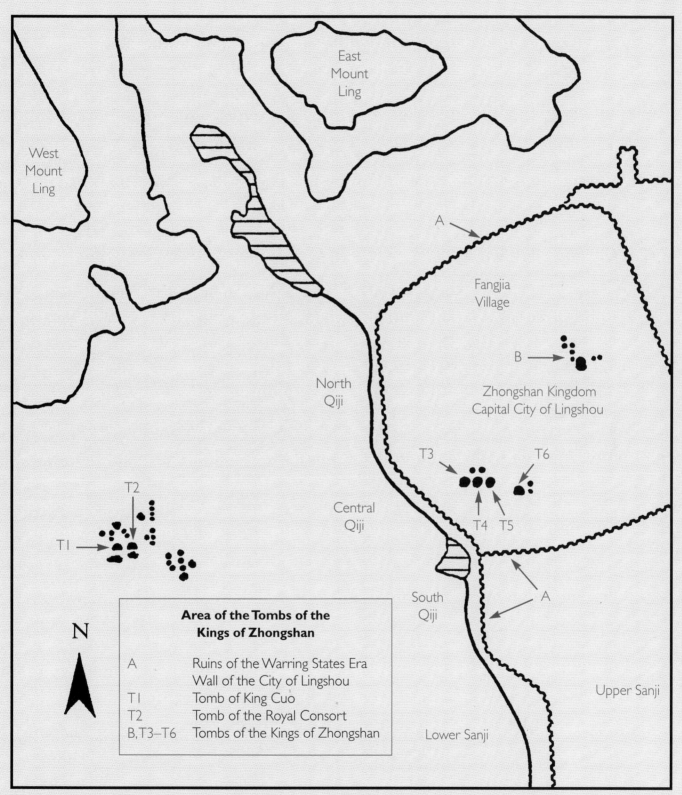

Figure I: Map of the area of the tombs of the kings of Zhongshan, near the modern township of Sanji, Pingshan district, Hebei. The original capital of the Zhongshan state was located near modern Ding district, Hebei, but was moved to Lingshou early in the fourth century B.C. Five generations of Zhongshan kings were buried here.

platform on the southern section (FIG. 2-A), and places for water drainage along the side of the first level.

The principal burial chamber in the T I tomb can be divided into six sections: the southern and northern passageways (FIGS. 2-B, 2-C), the chamber housing the coffin (FIG. 2-D), and the northeastern, eastern, and western treasuries (FIGS. 2-E, 2-F, 2-G, respectively). Of these, the central chamber housing the coffin and the northeastern treasury had been robbed clean, but the eastern and western treasuries had not. The central chamber was filled with rocks and contained two outer and two inner coffins, a few small decorative objects, a large amount of pottery, and strands of beads made of bone. The most important object in the tomb was a bronze fire-damaged plaque depicting the "Auspicious World" (*zhaoyutu*). It is 36.6 inches long, 18.7 inches wide, and 0.39 inches thick. One side was decorated with a pair of animal heads; cast-inlaid in gold and silver on the other side was an illustration of the "Auspicious World."

The plaque, an elaborate plan for the burial district, gave the location of the outer walls and the areas of the tombs, as well as the name of each unit of the construction, its size, placement, and the original decree of the king of Zhongshan. The decree stated that the prescribed dimensions were to be followed in the construction of the tomb, and that any problem that arose would be dealt with according to the law. Anyone who disobeyed the law was to be executed without pardon, and those who failed to carry out the king's order were to have their punishment extended to their children and grandchildren.

One of these plaques was buried in the tomb, another was stored in the king's palace. It is the oldest architectural site plan in East Asia. Although only two were completed, the original plan called for five tombs for the king and his consorts. Architectural renderings of the funerary park as it would have appeared (FIG. 3) show it to be a precursor of the vast burial complex of the First Emperor, Qinshihuang.

Relics in the eastern and western treasuries are numerous. The eastern treasury, 38 feet long, 10.5 feet wide, and 10 feet deep, was constructed of packed earth and contained a wooden coffin. Among the objects excavated was a set of lacquered vessels that included a *ding*, a *hu*, a *pan*, and a box. Among the bronze vessels were a *pan* with a hawk on a column, a cylindrical vessel, and a set of small *hu*, a square-shaped *hu*, a round *hu*, a *ding*, a *pan*, a bowl, a wash basin, a box, a winnower, a frame for curtains, a table with four deer, four dragons, and four phoenixes inlaid in gold and silver, fifteen lanterns, a divine beast with a pair of wings inlaid in silver, a base for a screen in the form of a tiger biting a deer with gold and silver decoration, a rhinoceros inlaid with gold and silver, a bronze ox inlaid with gold and silver, and an iron heating basin.

The western treasury is 20.8 feet long, 15.5 feet wide, and 9.8 feet deep. It also contained a coffin. Among the objects excavated are nine *ding*, an inlaid *ding*, a round *hu*, a square *hu*, a *gui*, a *li*, a spoon, a bell, a divine beast with a pair of wings inlaid with silver, and an iron heating basin,

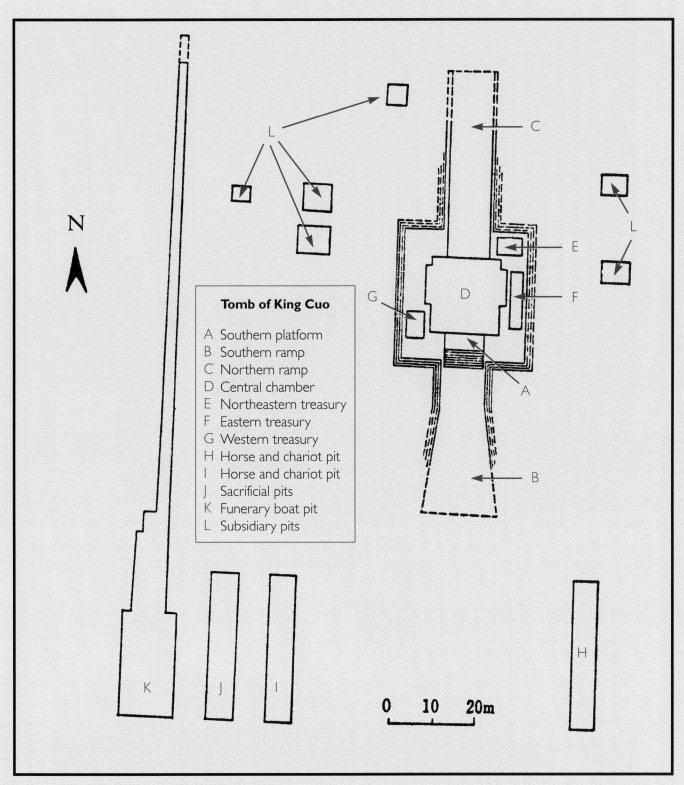

Tomb of King Cuo

A Southern platform
B Southern ramp
C Northern ramp
D Central chamber
E Northeastern treasury
F Eastern treasury
G Western treasury
H Horse and chariot pit
I Horse and chariot pit
J Sacrificial pits
K Funerary boat pit
L Subsidiary pits

N

0   10   20m

Figure 2: Plan of the tomb of King Cuo of Zhongshan.

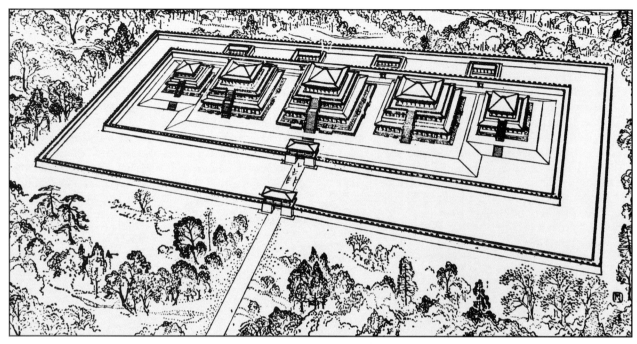

Figure 3: Artist's rendering of King Cuo of Zhongshan's massive burial park as it might have appeared had it been completed. Of the five tiled-roof pavilions planned for the king and his wives and concubines, only two were finished, those of the king and his royal consort. The drawing is based on a burial site plan inscribed on a bronze plaque discovered in the tomb.

as well as a set of pottery ritual vessels, crystal objects, and jade objects. These jade objects number more than 350, and some still bear inscriptions in ink.

At the base of the tomb are two pits, one to the east and one to the west, which contained chariots and horses (FIGS. 2-H, 2-I). Along the side of the base are pits with various other sacrificial burials (FIG. 2-J), including one with a funerary boat (FIG. 2-K). Most of the six subsidiary pits (FIG. 2-L) had been robbed, and only an inner and outer coffin remained in each. The heads of these coffins faced the principal tomb, indicating that they must have held the wives and concubines of the individual in the T1 tomb.

The chariot and horse pits symbolized the power of the state of Zhongshan. Each is approximately 111 feet long and 12 feet wide, and each contained the bones of twelve horses, as well as chariots, three-pronged halberds, an assortment of weapons, and tent poles. Of the four chariots in each, two at the southern end were drawn by four horses each, and two in the northern area were drawn by two horses each. Inside the chariots were objects such as bamboo quivers, bamboo arrowheads, bronze swords, bronze axes, bronze daggers, rattan-covered iron staves, and a gold dagger ferrule with a dragon design. Some of the chariots also contained bronze crossbows, and four bronze bells had been placed behind the two chariots in the northern area.

Two pits with various sacrifices were located alongside FIG. 2-J that contained objects used by the principal occupant of the tomb in connection with hunting. Similar in size, these pits together contained ten goats, six horses, three chariots, and two hunting dogs. The collars of the hunting dogs were made of gold and silver, indicating the luxurious lifestyle of King Cuo of Zhongshan.

The burial pit containing a boat, located to the west of the pits with various sacrificial objects, is highly unusual. The surface area has a protruding shape like the ideograph *tu* (土), "earth," and north of this a trough was dug to represent a river. Three large boats were placed on the south side of the pit, and a smaller boat was placed on either side of these. The territory of the state of Zhongshan stretched along the Taihang Mountains and was landlocked; there were no lakes, and no border along the Yellow River. Why these boats were buried remains a mystery.

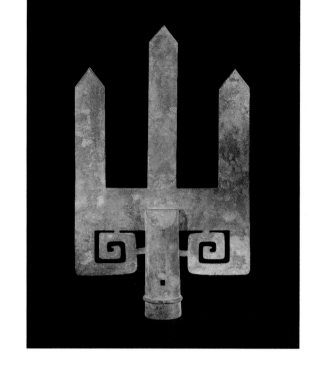

TWO BRONZE THREE-PRONGED STANDARDS IN THE SHAPE OF A HALBERD

Height 119 cm (46.4 in)
Weight of each piece 56 kg (123.8 lb)

Excavated in 1978 from the tomb of King Cuo
of Zhongshan in Pingshan district, Hebei

Hebei Research Institute of Cultural Relics

Five bronze three-pronged standards were excavated from King Cuo's tomb. Inscribed on one of them, however, is the number "7," so evidently more than five were originally buried. The missing two may have been buried in the first of the two pits with chariots and horses, which was robbed. The standards are in the shape of the ideograph "*shan*" (山), "mountain." The center of the lower portion is a round barrel. When excavated, the barrel contained charcoal, indicating that the halberd was originally mounted on a wooden pole. It has the shape of a large bronze halberd and therefore is called a "Three-Pronged Standard in the Shape of a Halberd." This may have been a ritual object symbolizing the power of the king.

BRONZE AX (*YUE*) OF THE MARQUIS OF ZHONGSHAN WITH CAP AND FINIAL

Length 29.6 cm (11.5 in); weight 2.4 kg (5.3 lb)

Excavated in 1978 from the tomb of King Cuo of Zhongshan in Pingshan district, Hebei

Hebei Research Institute of Cultural Relics

According to the dictionary *Explanation of Ideographs* by Xu Shen (A.D. 30–124) of the Eastern Han dynasty, "A *yue* is a large ax," indicating that the *yue* was a development of the common ax (*fu*). A gift from the Zhou king, to whom regional monarchs still paid homage, this bronze *yue* was a symbol of King Cuo's authority and commemorates the bestowal upon him of the title Marquis. It bears the inscription, "The Son of Heaven has established the realm and the Marquis of Zhongshan supports it. This ax was manufactured that his people may respect him."

An image of a cormorant, a fish, and a stone ax was found painted on a large Neolithic pottery jar excavated in the district of Linru, Henan. Research indicates that the jar was a burial object belonging to a tribal chief, and the painted stone ax probably represents one owned by the chief when he was alive. Evidence such as this suggests that the ax was a symbol of political power early in primitive society.

In addition to its use in warfare and in executions, the *yue* also functioned as a symbol of royal power. Among the earliest inscriptions on oracle bones excavated at Yinxu in Anyang are ideographs for "king" (王), some of which resemble the shapes of axes. In the beginning of a certain year in the eleventh century B.C., King Wu of the Zhou led an army northward across the

Yellow River. On a plain outside the Shang dynasty capital of Chaoge, the king harangued his troops, proclaiming the evil deeds of King Zhou of the Shang. At this time, King Wu held a bronze *yue* in his left hand and a white war flag in his right hand. After the army of King Zhou was defeated and he immolated himself in his palace, King Wu used the bronze *yue*, which he held in his hand as a symbol of royal authority, to decapitate King Zhou and hung the head above the white flag. He also used a black *yue* to decapitate King Zhou's favorite concubine, Danji, and hung her head above a smaller white flag.

When later kings and emperors ventured out on tours of inspection, axes were carried in their carriages to symbolize their majesty. In the chapter "Regulations of the King" in the *Book of Ritual* (*Liji*: "Wangzhi"), it was written that "bows and arrows are bestowed on the various nobles before they set out on a campaign, and iron axes are bestowed on them before they go forth to kill." Inscriptions on bronze vessels of the Western Zhou (ca. eleventh century–771 B.C.) often refer to the Zhou king's practice of bestowing bows and axes upon those who gain merit in battle. The intention behind this is to grant them the authority to kill, and to empower them to carry out military campaigns on behalf of the king.

BRONZE STAND IN THE SHAPE OF A TIGER BITING A DEER WITH DESIGNS CAST IN GOLD AND SILVER

Height 21.9 cm (8.5 in)
Length 51 cm (19.9 in)
Weight 26.6 kg (58.8 lb)

Excavated in 1977 from the tomb of
King Cuo of Zhongshan in Pingshan district, Hebei

Hebei Research Institute of Cultural Relics

This is a stand for a screen in the form of a ferocious spotted tiger holding a fawn it has caught in its mouth. The tiger's body is stretched like a bow as it walks, and its tail resembles a long sword curled at the tip. Fierce in appearance, the tiger bites the fawn's waist while using its right paw to grasp the fawn's leg. The fawn twists its neck to look back, while its legs are bent in a vain struggle that perfectly depicts the powerful consuming the weak.

The bodies of both tiger and fawn are decorated with designs cast in gold and silver, including stripes and geometric patterns, endowing the piece with even greater liveliness and beauty.

BRONZE RHINOCEROS SCREEN STAND
WITH DESIGNS CAST IN GOLD AND SILVER

Height 22.1 cm (8.6 in); length 55.5 cm (21.6 in); weight 19.4 kg (42.8 lb)

Excavated in 1978 from the tomb of King Cuo
of Zhongshan in Pingshan district, Hebei

Hebei Research Institute of Cultural Relics

This bronze rhinoceros screen stand is covered with designs cast in gold and silver, and bears a rectangular cylinder in the shape of an animal mask. A wood support remains in the barrel of the cylinder. The stand is quite heavy in order to support the weight of the screen. It was excavated with the bronze stand of a tiger biting a deer and a bronze ox screen stand with designs cast in gold and silver. Ancient Chinese customarily sat on mats, and screens were frequently used to divide space in a room. The scale of these objects indicates that they were designed to accommodate people who would have been sitting or kneeling on mats.

**BRONZE DIVINE WINGED ANIMAL
WITH DESIGNS CAST IN GOLD AND SILVER**

Height 24.6 cm (9.6 in); length 40.5 cm (15.8 in)

Excavated in 1977 from the tomb of King Cuo of
Zhongshan in Pingshan district, Hebei

Hebei Research Institute of Cultural Relics

This divine animal resembles the mythical *bixie*
beast of the later Han dynasty and is probably a
forerunner of those creatures. Its body is covered
in flower designs cast in gold and silver.

   This is the earliest example of such a
strange animal. After this, a large number of
strange animals appeared from the Han through
the Wei-Jin (A.D. 220–420) dynasties. The largest,
placed in front of tombs, were carved in stone
and weighed several tons, while the smallest were
hand-sized jade objects. All displayed horns on

their heads and had wings protruding from their
ribs. Human imagination has often equated
divinity with flight, and divine beings and
animals, celestial horses, and divine dragons were
all given wings.

   The people of the Han dynasty called
these animals "*bixie*" or "*tianlu*" (emolument from
Heaven). The ideographs for *bixie* mean "driving
away evil influences," so this divine animal must
have been used to ward off evil and in prayers for
blessings.

CYLINDRICAL BRONZE VESSEL WITH RHINOCEROS FEET AND COILED SERPENT PATTERNS

Height 58.8 cm (22.9 in)
Diameter of mouth 24.5 cm (9.5 in)
Weight 39.6 kg (87.5 lb)

Excavated in 1977 from the tomb
of King Cuo of Zhongshan in
Pingshan district, Hebei

Hebei Research Institute of Cultural Relics

The function of this cylindrical vessel is not clear and no similar object has yet been found. Three equidistant rhinoceroses form the feet and support the flat-bottomed cylinder, which is encircled by a wide belt design. There are stylized serpent patterns on the outside of the cylinder, and on both sides is an animal head biting a ring.

BRONZE BASIN (*PEN*) WITH A COLUMN BEARING A HAWK

Height 46.8 cm (18.2 in)
Diameter 60 cm (23.4)

Excavated in 1977 from the tomb
of King Cuo of Zhongshan
in Pingshan district, Hebei

Hebei Research Institute of Cultural Relics

Supporting this bronze basin is a column joined to a round base with a carved design of coiled serpents. Soldered equidistantly on the outside of the basin are four flying hawks, each of which holds a ring through a loop in its neck. On the bottom surface of the basin is a climbing turtle bearing a column on its back; on top of this column is a hawk grasping a pair of snakes. The hawk, stretching its wings and about to take flight, appears alive and exuberant.

The innovative form of this basin displays unique artisanship. Inscribed on the base is the date of the casting, as well as the names of the artisans involved.

Cultural Relics Excavated from the Pits Containing Soldier and Horse Figures at the
Tomb of the First Emperor of Qin
(Qinshihuang, r. 246–210 B.C.)

In March, 1974, peasants were digging a well in a persimmon-tree grove south of the village of Xiyang in China's northern Shaanxi province. When they dug down six feet, they found pieces of terracotta. When they reached eleven feet, they came upon the head of a "pottery man." The discovery was immediately reported to the proper authorities, and a team of government archaeologists was organized to excavate the site. It was soon learned that the well diggers had stumbled upon one of the greatest archaeological discoveries of all time: a spectacular burial guard, now thought to number as many as 8,000 terracotta soldiers, chariots, and horses, at the tomb of the First Emperor, Qinshihuang (259–210 B.C.).

Qinshihuang came to the throne as Ying Zheng, ruler of the state of Qin, the most powerful of the states vying for dominance at the end of the Warring States period. In the decade from 230 to 221 B.C., the armies of Qinshihuang conquered the Warring States of Han, Zhao, Wei, Chu, Yan, and Qi, establishing China's first unified state. An authoritarian ideology was promoted, strict laws and cruel punishments were carried out, a common currency and standards of measurement were introduced, and taxes and forced labor became heavy burdens. The Great Wall was built, and vast highway and construction projects were begun. The population of the country at the time of unification has been estimated at 20 million. More than two million— one tenth of the entire population—were conscripted for military campaigns or forced to build the Great Wall, the fortifications on the Five Ridges, the Ebang Palace, and the First Emperor's tomb at Mount Li (Lishan).

Construction of the vast funerary park at Lishan continued for some forty years, from the emperor's accession to the throne at thirteen until the fall of the Qin kingdom in 206 B.C., four years after his death at forty-nine. One hundred years later, the Western Han historian Sima Qian would write that 700,000 workers were conscripted to build the tomb after unification in 221 B.C. The tomb lies 3 miles east of the modern administrative center of Lintong district, north of Mount Li and south of the Wei River. Based on excavations and archaeological estimates, the central tumulus occupies an area of approximately 22 square miles and was originally bordered by rectangular inner and outer walls. The inner wall extends 1,918 feet from east to west and 4,428 feet from north to south. The outer wall extends 3,083 feet from east to west and 7,101 feet from north to south, with gates on all four sides of its 3.85-mile perimeter and an observation tower at each corner. The tumulus lies within the southern portion of the inner wall. Measured from the bottom of the stele at its northern edge, the tumulus presently stands at 156 feet in the shape of an overturned dipper. It is thought to have been a 400-foot-high four-sided pyramid planted with trees to make it look like a mountain. Beneath the tumulus is the as-yet-unexcavated underground palace (*digong*) containing the coffin of Qinshihuang.

The archaeological workers began by investigating the area at the well, which lies about one mile east of the tomb. They gradually discovered several pits of figures, numbered I to 4 in the order of their discovery. The pits are 16.4 to 23 feet deep and divided into corridors by double walls running from east to west, forming what are called "tunnels" (*guodong*). The figures of soldiers and horses stand in military formation in the tunnels, the floors of which were covered with green tiles. A wooden structure was originally built over the trenches and its roof hidden beneath 10 feet of earth, but the structure is thought to have burned and collapsed when the tomb was looted at the fall of the dynasty.

The entire pit area covers $5^{1}/_{2}$ acres. Pit No. I is the largest, measuring approximately 700 feet long, 200 feet across, and 14,000 square yards in area. Pit No. 2 has an "L" shape like a carpenter's square and is 7,200 square yards in area. Pit No. 3 is shaped like the ideograph "*ao*" (凹), "depression," and covers 624 square yards. Pit No. 4, located between Pits 2 and 3, is rectangular and covers 4,800 square yards. At present, Pit No. 3 has been completely excavated; Pit Nos. I and 2 have only been partially excavated. Pit No. 4 is empty and was apparently abandoned before completion.

Pit I is the most thoroughly studied, containing an estimated 6,000 life-sized terracotta soldiers, horses, and chariots. It consists of eleven trenches running east to west the length of the pit and one north-to-south aisle at each end. A vanguard of unarmored archers and bowmen occupies the eastern north-to-south aisle; of these, the three tallest figures appear to be officers. Behind them, at the heads of six of the trenches, are chariot groups consisting of four horses and

eighteen soldiers, followed by thirty-six rows of infantry.

The height of the pottery soldiers ranges from 5.6 to 6.2 feet; the horses are approximately 5 feet tall and 6.5 feet long. Most of the soldiers once held real weapons, including long-distance bows, crossbows, and arrows. The long weapons include spears, halberds, long daggers, and staves. The short weapons include swords and scimitars, as well as ritual axes. All of these weapons were cast in bronze. After undergoing chromium oxidation anticorrosion treatment, they are still sharp and glisten like new despite more than two thousand years in the earth.

The second pit, although only partially excavated, is believed to have been manned by an estimated 1,300 figures arranged in formations of archers, bowmen, infantry, cavalry, and chariots. Pit No. 3 contains high-ranking officers and one chariot and may have represented the elite command center of the First Emperor's army.

The main body of soldiers and horses faces east in precise, tight military formation. Some researchers believe that the formations reflect actual battle arrangements used by the Qin army. The arrangement in Pit No. I is a joint force of Qin infantry and chariot units. Pit No. 2 is a combined unit of infantry, chariots, and cavalry. Pit No. 3 represents the high command. Magnificent and martial, they illustrate the frightening scene that exists before battle.

In December, 1980, additional pits were discovered beyond the western wall of the underground palace. Placed one behind the other in one of the pits were a bronze half-sized chariot and a half-sized carriage with horses. Outside of the western gate of the inner wall was a pit covering 2,400 square yards. In it were buried many pottery coffins containing the bones of exotic birds and animals that had been part of the imperial zoo. North of the pit for birds and animals was an area where a large structure once stood. Inscriptions such as "Belonging to the Officials in Charge of Food at Mount Li" were found on pottery vessels there, indicating that this was where food offerings and sacrifices were made to the emperor.

North of the underground palace lie the remains of the foundation of the Hall of Slumber (*Qindian*), built as a habitation for the soul of the emperor. Here, clothing, objects for the honor guard, and objects for daily use were set out. East of the outer wall are other royal tombs of the Qin dynasty, as well as tombs of important officials buried after death to accompany the emperor.

The artistry of the pottery sculpture of the Qin, designed as a form of commemoration, conveys a powerful sense of the era. The most important aesthetic characteristics are realism, technical discipline, clear representation of individual character, and animated form. The expressions, clothing, and ornaments of the terracotta soldiers and horses were carefully copied from life. The soldiers' top-knots, tied in many different ways, belt buckles fastened to belts, cobbled soles on the bottoms of their shoes, and the saddles and saddle cloths worn by the horses

are all represented in faultless detail. The expressive faces were designed to endow the Qin figures with many different personalities. The intricate carving of the symmetrical eyebrows, nostrils, lips, and whiskers solemnly captures the bravery of the generals and soldiers, their impassiveness and quick intelligence, and their martial strength. From pigments found on the figures, it is clear that they were brightly painted in green, vermilion, pink, purple, blue, yellow, orange, gray, brown, black, and white. The horses were painted in a roan color with pink on the ears, nostrils, and gums. The faces, hands, and feet of the soldiers were pink, while clothing was done in contrasting colors. Eyebrows and whiskers were indicated in black. Originally, the pupils of the eyes were carved to protrude. When the eyes were painted and clearly distinguished in black and white, a spirited, realistic effect was achieved, calling to mind the story of the painted dragon that came alive and flew away when the pupils of its eyes were dotted.

Several pottery-figure workshop areas have been located near the pits. Based on research into the method of manufacture, it can be concluded that the figures were sculpted, molded in separate pieces, and assembled individually, then further sculpted, fired in a kiln, and painted after firing—an assembly-line process that required the efforts of hundreds of artisans and laborers.

POTTERY FIGURE OF A GENERAL

Height 190 cm (74.1 in)

Excavated in 1976 from Pit No. 2
at the tomb of Qinshihuang
in Lintong district, Shaanxi

Museum of Terracotta Warriors and
Horses of Qinshihuang, Shaanxi

Excavated from Pit No. 2 in 1976, this figure
wears a uniform beneath an intricate and
distinctive set of armor tied around his shoulders,
chest, and back with a colored sash. Protective
leggings cover his shins, and he wears sandals with
rectangular openings and raised toes. His arms are
crossed in front of his abdomen and his hands are
positioned to rest on a sword. He has a square
face, broad forehead, large mouth with thick lips,
and a mustache in the shape of the ideograph
"*ba*" (八), "eight"—a typical man of Qin from
the Guanzhong area. The sculptor did not try
to represent a domineering manner but rather
showed him in an attitude of profound
contemplation of strategy. He looks downward
with slightly arched brows, giving the appearance
of a resolute, steadfast, self-possessed, and highly
intelligent Confucian general with many plans
in mind.

POTTERY FIGURE OF A MILITARY OFFICER

Height 190 cm (74.1 in)

Excavated in 1974 from Pit No. 1
at the tomb of Qinshihuang
in Lintong district, Shaanxi

Museum of Terracotta Warriors and
Horses of Qinshihuang, Shaanxi

This pottery figure of a military officer wears
armor but no helmet. The soldiers of Qin went
into battle without helmets and were marked by
unparalleled bravery. His eyes are firmly fixed, and
he appears calm. He wears a rectangular cap and a
long coat beneath armor that resembles fish scales.
His legs are wrapped in protective leggings. His
right arm is straight with the hand slightly bent,
while the left arm is curved and the hand modeled
to grasp a weapon. He appears to belong to the
middle ranks of Qin military officers.

POTTERY FIGURE OF A MILITARY OFFICER

Height 183 cm (71.3 in)

Excavated in 1974 from Pit No. 1
at the tomb of Qinshihuang
in Lintong district, Shaanxi

Museum of Terracotta Warriors and
Horses of Qinshihuang, Shaanxi

This is the image of a low ranking Qin officer. He
wears a round top-knot and a round soft cap. His
shins are protected by leggings, and he wears
square-toed shoes. The half-closed hands
originally held weapons.

POTTERY FIGURE OF A WARRIOR

Height 178 cm (69.4 in)

Excavated in 1976 from Pit No. I
at the tomb of Qinshihuang
in Lintong district, Shaanxi

Museum of Terracotta Warriors and
Horses of Qinshihuang, Shaanxi

This figure has finely detailed hair combed back
into a secured braid. A coat of armor covers his
shoulders and torso. His left hand is straight, and
his right hand is half-closed and once held a
weapon. He wears square-toed sandals laced up
with cords.

IMPERIAL
TOMBS
OF CHINA
中国皇陵

POTTERY CHARIOT HORSE

Height 172 cm (67 in); length 205 cm (80 in)

Excavated in 1979 from Pit No. I
at the tomb of Qinshihuang
in Lintong district, Shaanxi

Museum of Terracotta Warriors and
Horses of Qinshihuang, Shaanxi

Throughout the Warring States period, the finest pulling horses came from Qin. The origin of the Qin horses was recorded in "Basic Annals of Qin" in *Historical Records* (*Shiji*: "Qin benji"), the first-century B.C. work by Sima Qian, the great Han dynasty court historian. During the time of King Xiao of the Zhou (ca. 900 B.C.), Feizi, an ancestor of the Qin, gained fame for his superior horse breeding. He was commanded to go to the Plain of Qianwei (to the west of modern Guanzhong, Shaanxi) to breed improved horses for the king of Zhou and was granted the region as a fief. From then on, the house of Qin prospered.

This powerful chariot horse seems to strain forward, bearing its teeth, as if pulling a chariot. Its tail has been tied to keep it clear of the harnesses.

BRONZE SPEARHEAD (*PI*)

Length 35 cm (13.6 in)

Excavated in 1976 from Pit No. I at the tomb
of Qinshihuang in Lintong district, Shaanxi

Museum of Terracotta Warriors and
Horses of Qinshihuang, Shaanxi

The surface of this spearhead is decorated with a
cloud pattern. The upper portion is similar to a
short sword and has a hexagonal faceted blade.

BRONZE CROSSBOW MECHANISM

Length 8 cm (3.I in)
Height 16.2 cm (6.3 in)

Excavated in 1979 from Pit No. I
at the tomb of Qinshihuang
in Lintong district, Shaanxi

Shaanxi Provincial Museum of
Soldier and Horse Figures
from the Tomb of Qinshihuang

This was the mechanized section of the crossbow
attached to the end of a wooden arm. An
important long-distance weapon of the Qin army,
the crossbow had become a standard weapon by
the fifth century B.C., more than I,200 years
before it was introduced in Europe.

TEN BRONZE ARROWHEADS

Length of each 17.2–20 cm (6.7–7.8 in)

Excavated in 1976 from Pit No. I at the tomb of
Qinshihuang in Lintong district, Shaanxi

Shaanxi Provincial Museum of Soldier and Horse Figures
from the Tomb of Qinshihuang

These bronze tips were attached to wooden or
bamboo shafts. More than 10,000 such
arrowheads have been excavated near the terracotta soldiers.

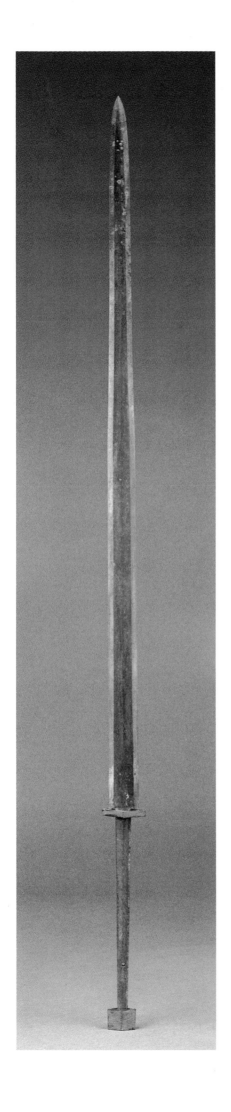

BRONZE SWORD

Length 91.5 cm (35.6 in)

Excavated in 1981 from Pit No. 1
at the tomb of Qinshihuang
in Lintong district, Shaanxi

Museum of Terracotta Warriors and
Horses of Qinshihuang, Shaanxi

A common weapon in the Qin army, this sword
still gleams as if it were new. It has a long, slim
body with ridges on both sides. The tip is sharp,
and the blade is faceted like a caltrop. Along the
flat surface of the blade is a slanting, filed pattern;
at the base is a round hole, and the sword guard is
also shaped like a caltrop. The handle is an oval
cylinder, and at the end of the handle is a cap.
Swords of this type often had inlays of turquoise,
jade, gold, or silver added at the guard.

Relics from the
Tombs of Imperial and Aristocratic Families
of the Han (206 B.C.–A.D. 220), Tang (618–906), and Liao (907–1125) Dynasties

BRONZE FIGURE OF A MOUNTED EMISSARY

Han dynasty

Height 54 cm (21 in)
Length 34 cm (13.2 in)

Excavated in 1969 from the Han dynasty tomb
at Lingtai in Wuwei, Gansu

Gansu Provincial Museum

In 1969, a Han dynasty tomb at Lingtai was
discovered along the old Silk Road in the city of
Wuwei in Gansu province. The occupant of the
tomb was a general surnamed Zhang during the
Eastern Han dynasty (A.D. 25–220). His tomb
was an imposing 131 feet long and 33 feet wide.
Although it had been robbed quite early, more
than two hundred funerary objects still remained,
including nearly one hundred bronze chariots,
horses, and honor guard figurines.

Among the horses and chariots excavated
from the tomb at Lingtai, this bronze figure of a
mounted emissary was the leader of a group of
armed cavalry in the honor guard. He rides a large
special breed with raised head and elevated tail.
His expression is serious. He holds a whip in his
left hand, and differs from other soldiers in that
he wears a large hat decorated with two horns to
denote higher status. Mounted cavalry had been
developed in the Warring States period but
achieved great power during the Han dynasty. The
saddle lacks a blanket or stirrups; the latter did
not appear until the fourth century under the
Northern and Southern dynasties.

BRONZE CAVALRY HORSE

Han dynasty

Height 39 cm (15.2 in)
Length 37 cm (14.4 in)

Excavated in 1969 from the Han dynasty tomb
at Lingtai in Wuwei, Gansu

Gansu Provincial Museum

This bronze principal horse is the mount for the
occupant of the tomb. Tall and large, and with a
dignified attitude, it follows behind the principal
chariot in the honor guard. The right front hoof
is placed slightly forward as it slowly proceeds. On
the horse's back is a saddle blanket made from flat
pieces of bronze. A horse galloping through the
clouds was painted on both sides of the blanket,
alluding to the fast, superior breed of horses such
as this one which came from Central Asia and
were known as "Celestial Horses" (*Tianma*).

BRONZE MOUNTED CAVALRYMAN HOLDING A HALBERD

Han dynasty

Height 55 cm (21.4 in)
Length 33 cm (12.8 in)

Excavated in 1969 from the Han dynasty tomb at Lingtai in Wuwei, Gansu

Gansu Provincial Museum

A combination of the dagger and the spear, the halberd is an ancient Chinese weapon requiring special skills. As this cavalryman rides among the honor guard of horses and chariots, his left hand grasps the reins and his right hand holds the halberd.

BRONZE MOUNTED CAVALRYMAN HOLDING A SPEAR

Han dynasty

Height 54 cm (21 in)
Length 33 cm (12.8 in)

Excavated in 1969 from the Han dynasty tomb at Lingtai in Wuwei, Gansu

Gansu Provincial Museum

Spear-carrying cavalrymen were also in the honor guard formation, located behind those holding halberds.

BRONZE CAVALRY HORSE

Han dynasty

Height 39 cm (15.2 in); length 37 cm (14.4 in)

Excavated in 1969 from the Han dynasty tomb
at Lingtai in Wuwei, Gansu, Gansu Provincial Museum

This bronze cavalry horse accompanies the tomb occupant's principal horse. It follows behind the principal horse (*above, page 85*) and represents the cavalry accompanying the occupant of the tomb.

Slightly smaller than the principal horse, it was cast in a graceful attitude with its mouth wide open and an elevated tail. Its front hoof is raised as if the horse were about to race ahead.

BRONZE CHARIOT WITH AX BEARER

Han dynasty

Height of horse 39 cm (15.2 in)
Length of chariot and horse 55 cm (21.4 in)
Width of chariot 41 cm (16 in)

Excavated in 1969 from the Han dynasty tomb
at Lingtai in Wuwei, Gansu

Gansu Provincial Museum

This bronze chariot with ax bearer is one of the leaders in the honor guard. Both shafts of the chariot curve upward and are connected to the horizontal harness. Each wheel has a double hub and twelve spokes. Lozenge shapes have been carved into the floor of the chariot to represent woven bamboo and rattan. The ax is the *yue* type, a symbol of political power in ancient China.

According to the "Treatise on Chariots and Clothing" in the *History of the Eastern Han Dynasty* (*Houhanshu*: "Yufuzhi"), an ax-bearing chariot may precede officials with the rank of a thousand piculs—the measure used to determine salaries paid in grain—and above. This represents the authority of the occupant of the tomb to carry out executions.

BRONZE LIGHT CARRIAGE

Han dynasty

Height 44 cm (17.1 in)
Length of carriage and horse 55 cm (21.4 in)
Width of carriage 41 cm (16 in)

Excavated in 1969 from the Han dynasty tomb
at Lingtai in Wuwei, Gansu

Gansu Provincial Museum

In contrast to a war chariot, which was pulled by
four horses, a light carriage (*yaoche*) was a small
carriage drawn by a single horse. This light
carriage is one of those leading the honor guard
of bronze chariots and horses. Like the ax-bearing
chariot, the shafts of the light chariot curve
upward and are joined to the horizontal harness;
each wheel has a double hub and twelve spokes. In
the middle of the carriage is a round canopy. A
driver is seated on the left side of the carriage, his
two hands held out in front of his chest as though
driving. Originally, red fabric was hung as a
curtain on both sides of the carriage. This
signifies that the occupant of the tomb was an
official above the rank of two thousand piculs.

TWO BRONZE TROOP LEADERS

Han dynasty

Height 22.3 cm (8.7 in)

Excavated in 1969 from the Han dynasty tomb
at Lingtai in Wuwei, Gansu

Gansu Provincial Museum

In ancient Chinese military regulations, the
smallest unit of five soldiers was called a "troop,"
and each troop had a leader. Troop leaders are also
called "troop leaders preceding the chariots," since
they ran before the chariots in the honor guard to
clear the way, lead the file, and serve as protection.
They originally held weapons such as knives or
staves, but these have not been preserved.

BRONZE LIGHT CARRIAGE

Han dynasty

Length 60 cm (23.4 in)

Excavated in 1969 from the Han dynasty tomb
at Lingtai in Wuwei, Gansu

Gansu Provincial Museum

This is another of the light carriages leading the procession but is slightly lower in status than its counterpart (*facing page*). On the breast of the horse is an inscription that reads, "The slave driver, horse, and light carriage of His Excellency Zhang, Commander of a Thousand Cavalry on the Left in Zhangye." This indicates that the carriage is for a relative of the occupant of the tomb, an official surnamed Zhang who held the rank of Commander of a Thousand Cavalry on the Left in Wuwei Commandery.

LARGE BRONZE HORSE

Han dynasty

Height 144 cm (56.1 in)
Length 70 cm (27.3 in)

Excavated in 1981 from Fangling village
in Xushui district, Hebei

Committee for the Preservation
of Cultural Relics of Baoding, Hebei

The mouth of this exquisite large bronze horse is
wide open, neighing in a pose typical of Han
dynasty horses. The head, ears, and legs were cast
individually and then assembled with the rest of
the body. On the face are two cast protrusions
from the bridge of the nose. The eye sockets and
nostrils are particularly pronounced, and the ears
are erect. Its firm, straight lines and powerful
stance express the vitality, majesty, and bravery of
Han dynasty horses.

During the reign of Emperor Wu of the
Han (141–87 B.C.) a superior breed of horse was
imported from the Western Region (the large area
west of Gansu) in order to improve the quality of
the horses of the Central Plains and counter the
onslaught of the powerful nomadic Xiongnu
tribes in the north. This bronze horse is another
exquisite model of these special breeds known as
"Celestial Horses."

BRONZE OPEN CARRIAGE

Han dynasty

Height 30 cm (11.7 in)
Length of carriage and horse 70 cm (27.3 in)
Width of carriage 33 cm (12.8 in)

Excavated in 1969 from the Han dynasty tomb
at Lingtai in Wuwei, Gansu

Gansu Provincial Museum

This bronze open carriage (*nian*) is one of
fourteen carriages in the bronze honor guard of
horses and chariots. When ridden by an official, it
was located at the very end of the honor guard
procession. Originally there was an awning frame
over the carriage, but this has not survived. An
inscription on the breast of the bronze horse
reads, "The horse and carriage of the late wife of
the commander of Zhangye with a slave carriage
leader and a maidservant." In the carriage are
bronze figurines of a slave driving the carriage and
a maidservant. The inscription makes it clear that
General Zhang had been commander of the
Zhangye area and that this carriage was to carry
his late wife.

TWO BRONZE MIRRORS

Han dynasty

1. Bronze Mirror with Design of
the King of the East (Dongwanggong) and
the Queen Mother of the West (Xiwangmu)

Diameter 19.2 cm (7.5 in)

Excavated from Yuejia village
in the northern suburbs of Loyang, Henan

Cultural Relics Excavation Team
of Loyang, Henan

Bronze mirrors were used by the ancient Chinese to cast their reflections. The reflecting surface is flat, shiny, and smooth, demonstrating the high level of accomplishment in the crafting of bronze mirrors in the Han dynasty. Around a protruding knob at the back of the mirror are images, decorations, and inscriptions. The base of the knob is decorated with patterns of lines and pearls; the images are separated by four smaller knobs. Carved in relief in opposite quadrants are the King of the East and the Queen Mother of the West, seated with folded hands in a solemn attitude and accompanied by attendants. Next to the images are the inscriptions "King" and "Queen Mother." The King and the Queen Mother are mythological characters symbolizing

longevity in ancient China. Opposite each other in the two remaining quadrants are a galloping horse and carriage and a tiger and leopard carved in relief. The carriage has a canopy and a seated driver. Around the band encircling the images is a cast inscription in clerical-style ideographs that reads, "Mr. Cai has manufactured this excellent mirror, brilliant as the moon, engraved with protective animals. It will bring wealth, nobility, and descendants. When you reach an advanced age, you will remain sound like metal and stone and not grow old but enjoy Heaven." Around the inscription are separate bands with patterns of rays, sawteeth, and clouds. The decorations are intricate and rich in content, indicating how people pursued the ideal of longevity.

On the back of this mirror in the center is a round knob with a pattern of four persimmon sepals around its base. The inscription "May You Always Be Granted Descendants" is engraved in seal-style characters between them. A sawtooth pattern around the edge of the mirror encircles a band divided into four quadrants by smaller knobs. Each quadrant contains two divine birds and animals facing each other in a dance. The lines of these designs are lively and graceful, and although some of the surface of the mirror is damaged by corrosion, it can still reflect a person's face clearly.

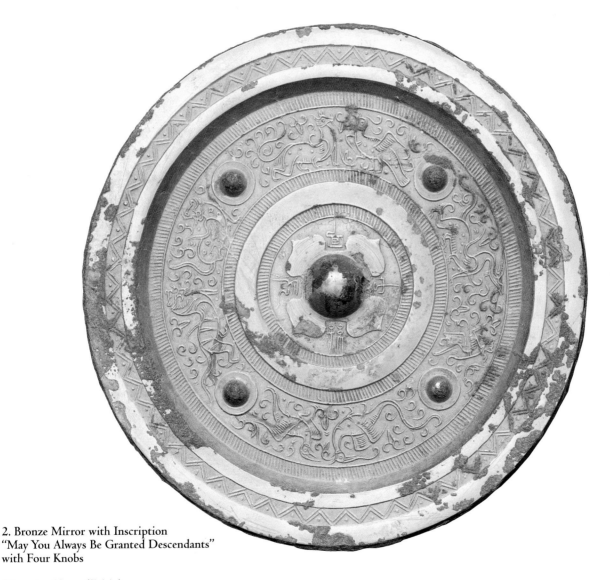

2. Bronze Mirror with Inscription
"May You Always Be Granted Descendants"
with Four Knobs

Diameter 19 cm (7.4 in)

Bureau of Cultural Relics and Gardening
of Xian, Shaanxi

GILT BRONZE LAMP IN THE SHAPE OF A RAM

Han dynasty

Height 19 cm (7.4 in)
Length 23 cm (8.9 in)

Bureau of Cultural Relics and Gardening
of Xian, Shaanxi

The body of this bronze lamp in the shape of a
ram is gilded. The ram's gaze is fixed straight
ahead, its four short legs tucked under. On its
back is a rectangular, movable cover attached to
the back of the neck. When opened and flipped
over onto the top of the head, it becomes the pan
for the lamp. The design of this ram-shaped lamp
is ingenious, simple, and pure. Practical as well as
beautiful, it alludes to the ideal of good fortune.

BRONZE LAMP IN THE FORM OF A GOOSE FOOT

Han dynasty

Height 22.2 cm (8.6 in)

**Bureau of Cultural Relics and Gardening
of Xian, Shaanxi**

This is a lamp for bright illumination. The column of the lamp is in the form of a goose foot. It supports the pan of the lamp, which is in the shape of a grooved ring with straight sides and a flat bottom. On the upper part of the column are swirling patterns on both sides. The goose foot rests on a base shaped like a horse hoof. The goose foot was a popular lamp style during the Han dynasty, and its popularity continued in later periods. It is celebrated in many Song dynasty (A.D. 960–1279) poems and essays, for example in the poem "Autumn Thoughts" from the collection *Poems from Jiannan* (*Jiannan shigao*: "Qiusi") by Lu Yu (1125–1210), the patriotic poet of the Southern Song: "My eyes are bright and can still make out characters the size of a fly's head; yet, as summer recedes, I've begun to draw nearer to the goose-footed lamp."

FOUR GILT BRONZE ANIMALS

Han dynasty

Length 4.5–7 cm (1.7–2.7 in)
Height 3.5–8.6 cm (1.3–3.3 in)

Excavated in 1974 from Yanshi district, Henan

Henan Provincial Museum

1. Gilt Bronze *Qilin*

The *qilin* is an auspicious animal in ancient Chinese folklore. This bronze *qilin* has a single horn on its raised head as it looks straight ahead. The entire body is gilded.

2. Gilt Bronze Water Buffalo

The horns on this bronze water buffalo turn inward; the body is strong, with a full, round waist. It is an image of the water buffalo commonly found in northern China.

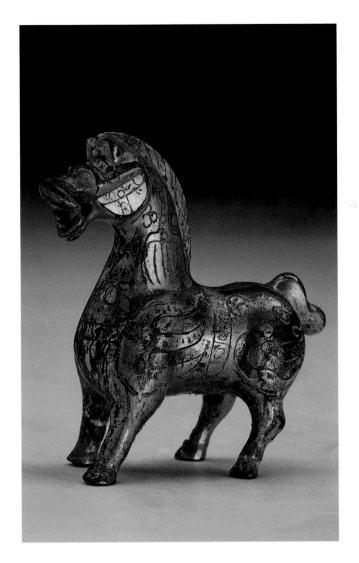

4. Gold and Silver Gilt Bronze Horse

This bronze horse is raising its head as it opens its mouth and neighs. Above its forward limbs are winglike designs while other parts bear patterns of curling clouds. The body is covered in both gold and silver, which is delicately wrought and highly attractive. The horse is a commonly depicted animal in Han dynasty art and the love of horses endured through both Han dynasties. It represents the importance of martial virtues among the ancient Chinese. One can see from the two wings on the shoulders of this gold and silver gilded bronze horse that it was a representation of the "Celestial Horses."

3. Gilt Bronze Elephant

This bronze elephant's trunk hangs down and curves inward. It is arched at the waist and its tail is flat against its body. Wild Asian elephants in China are now found only in the tropical rain forest of Yunnan province. However, in ancient China, they lived in the Yellow River area in Henan province. The literary abbreviation for Henan province is "Xiang," which means "place of great elephants."

JADE BURIAL SUIT WITH GOLD THREADS

Han dynasty

1. Jade Burial Suit with Gold Threads
   Length 176 cm (68.6 in)

2. Jade Nose Plugs
   Length 2.5 cm (1 in); diameter 1 cm (0.39 in)

3. Jade Ear Plug
   Length 1.6 cm (0.6 in); diameter 1 cm (0.39 in)

4. Jade Mouth Amulet
   Length 6.2 cm (2.4 in); width 3.3 cm (1.2 in)

Excavated from the tomb of Liu Sui, Prince of Liang, in Yongcheng district, Henan

Shangqiu City Museum, Henan

The Chinese long attributed magical properties to jade. During the Qin and Han periods, a shroud of jade was thought to protect royal remains from decay. In recent years, several such suits have been excavated from imperial and aristocratic tombs. This burial outfit of flat jade pieces sewn together with gold thread was tailored to the proportions of the deceased. It is composed of head and face coverings, a jacket, sleeves, gloves, pants, and foot coverings—eleven sections in all, using 2,007 pieces of jade and more than two pounds of gold thread. This jade came from Hezhen (Khotan) in Xinjiang.

It was also widely believed that plugging the "nine orifices" of the body with jade would prevent decay. Jade pieces were held in each hand, and were used as ear plugs, nose plugs, and eye coverings. A jade amulet, typically in the shape of a cicada, was placed in the mouth.

Only an emperor could wear a jade suit with gold threads. The *History of the Eastern Han Dynasty* (*Houhanshu*, early fifth century A.D.) records strict regulations concerning their use. Hereditary nobles and princes, newly enfeoffed nobles, worthy ladies, and princesses were allowed to wear jade suits with silver threads, while elder worthy ladies and senior princesses could wear jade suits with bronze threads.

Although known from ancient historical texts, the first jade burial suits to be discovered were found in the late sixties in Mancheng district, Hebei. This suit is one of about two dozen that have since been excavated in China. Its wearer was Liu Sui, Prince of Liang, who died in 39 B.C. during the Western Han dynasty. Although the prince belonged to the class of hereditary nobles and princes, he was buried in a jade suit with gold threads, probably because regulations regarding jade suits had not yet been established. The size and shape of each jade piece underwent careful design and intricate workmanship. The manufacture of the gold thread was also very precise, demonstrating a high level of craftsmanship. It has been estimated that ten years and many skilled artisans were required to produce a single jade suit. Only emperors, princes, and nobles could afford such luxury.

POTTERY TOWER

Han dynasty

Height 147 cm (57.3 in)

Excavated in 1952 from Chiunuzhong
(Tomb of Nine Women) in Huaiyang district, Henan

Henan Provincial Museum

Architecture was an accomplished art in Han China. The original wooden structures have disappeared, but tomb models give us a record of the construction skills and architectural styles of the period. Glazed pottery models of towers are often found in Han dynasty tombs. Although their funerary function is still unclear, descriptions of towers for military, agricultural, and entertainment purposes appear in literature of the time, and they also symbolized wealth and rank.

This example is considered among the most beautiful. Imposing and lavishly decorated, it is divided into three stories. On the ground floor are five people conversing. Behind a staircase in the shape of the ideograph "*ren*" (人), "man," are the two leaves of a front door decorated with stylized animal heads holding rings. The second and third stories contain couches but no people. The roof of the third story ends in curved eaves. On the roof are flat tiles, rounded tiles, and end tiles, all represented in detail. A large bird sits at the tip of each of the four eaves on each story; another large bird sits on the ridge of the roof of the third story. In all, there are thirteen large birds. Outside each of the pillars on the second and third stories are two statues of naked figures. Beneath the railings are more statues of small men. Altogether, there are fifty-two large and small statues of men.

103

POTTERY COURTYARD HOUSE

Han dynasty

Height 76 cm (29.6 in)
Width 90 cm (35.1 in)
Depth 85 cm (33.1 in)

Excavated in 1959 in Zhengzhou, Henan

Henan Provincial Museum

This is a model of the "enclosed courtyard house" popular among the common people, and one of the earliest models of its type. The plan consists of buildings on all four sides in the form of the ideograph "*kou*" (口), "mouth," and is comprised of six units: the gate, observation tower, storehouse, residential quarters, kitchen, outhouse, and pigsty. Inside the gate lies a household dog. Facing the doorway are the residential quarters. Five steps lead up to the raised floor. To the left is the kitchen. When excavated, it still contained models of a stir-frying pan, basin, and other cooking equipment. Opposite the kitchen is an observation tower. To the right of the residential quarters are the outhouse and pigsty. Chickens roost on top of the outhouse, and pigs are fattened in the pigsty. The storehouse stands opposite the outhouse and pigsty. A staircase in the shape of the ideograph "*ba*" (八), "eight," leads up to the storehouse, which has large windows to permit ventilation for the storage of grain.

This model of a courtyard house reflects the self-sufficient economy of the people as well as the architectural style of houses at this time.

SET OF SEVEN PAINTED POTTERY FIGURINES OF ENTERTAINERS

Han dynasty

Height 24 cm (9.3 in)
Length 28 cm (10.9 in)
Width 19 cm (7.4 in)

Excavated in 1972 in Zhangwan, Lingbao district, Henan

Henan Provincial Museum

This is a set of seven figurines of performing musicians and dancers. Four of the figurines play music, while a male and two female figurines dance. The male dancer wears a hat, and the upper portion of his body is bare as he sings and claps to keep time, one foot on the ground, the other raised. The female dancers have their hair done up in double chignons and wave their sleeves as they dance. Stepping on the bowl-shaped drums, they perform a dance of the time known as a "drum-stepping dance."

STONE INKSTONE WITH COILED DRAGONS

Han dynasty

Diameter 33.3 cm (12.9 in)
Height 18.2 cm (7 in)

Excavated in 1978 in Nanle district, Henan

Henan Provincial Museum

The use of inkstones was widespread by the Han dynasty and there have been many discoveries of Han inkstones in recent years. Few, however, can compare to the exquisite beauty of this rare and valuable stone carving. In the center of the cover is a round knob. In the middle of the spiral pattern is the ideograph "*jun*" (君), "noble," written in the clerical style. Coiled around the knob are six flying dragons whose heads meet at the knob as if they are competing to obtain a pearl. There are engraved patterns of a string of pearls, waves, spirals, and flowers around the edges of the cover and the inkstone. The inkstone rests on three feet carved in the shape of strange animals. Their ears are erect,

their eyes are round, and their mouths are wide open. Their claws seem to press on their knees as they support the inkstone with the strength of their shoulders.

The bottom of the inkstone is engraved with a round, swirling pattern in the middle of which is engraved, in two seal-style ideographs, "*wuzhu*" (五珠), "five pearls." In the center is a hollow. Toward one edge of the surface of the inkstone is an engraved cup amid a flower design. The inside of the cup is an oval-shaped concavity, next to which are two more concavities. These are probably intended for the balls of ink which were ground with water. An inscription is engraved

along the edge of the inkstone that reads, "In the third year of the *yanxi* era in *renchen*, the seventh lunar month, on *dingyou*, the seventh day, the noble Gao was raised to the rank of regional inspector with a salary of two thousand piculs. May this noble lord of lofty rank enjoy longevity like metal and stone and forever use this inkstone worth two thousand." This means that on August 26, A.D. 160, during the third year of the *yanxi* era of the Han emperor Huan, Gao, the owner of the inkstone, was promoted to regional inspector, which is roughly equivalent to the modern post of provincial governor, and that his salary was two thousand piculs of grain. As he had become an

important official of the court, the wish was made that he live as long as metal and stone endure and forever use this inkstone worth two thousand "qian," a traditional monetary unit. This inkstone was probably presented to him by his subordinates or disciples to congratulate him on his promotion. It was an extraordinarily high price for that time. The stone possesses a dignified, classic elegance and the carving is delicate. Its date endows it with a high degree of historical value.

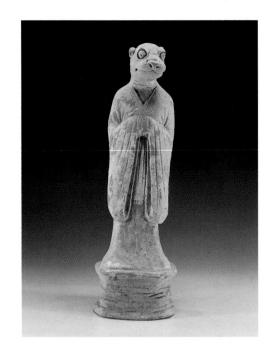

SET OF POTTERY FIGURINES OF THE TWELVE CALENDRICAL ANIMALS

Tang dynasty

Height 38–41.5 cm (14.8–16.1 in)

Excavated in 1955 from a Tang dynasty tomb in the suburbs of Xian, Shaanxi

The Historical Museum of Shaanxi

Hands folded across their chests, these twelve pottery figurines with human bodies and animal heads represent the Chinese twelve-year cycle in which each year is associated with a specific animal—rat, ox, tiger, rabbit, dragon, snake, horse, goat, monkey, chicken, dog, and pig. The twelve calendrical animals are also called the "twelve time-period," the "twelve astronomical animals," and the "twelve cyclical characters." Groups of twelve had appeared by the Warring States period, and the identity of the animals was fixed by the Han dynasty. The practice of

determining one's year of birth by the twelve cyclical characters first became popular during the Northern Zhou dynasty (557–581). By the Sui (581–618) and Tang dynasties, the twelve calendrical animals were widely engraved in varying styles on funerary steles and around the edges of epitaphs. The custom of calculating the year based on a horary cycle of sixty years (combining the twelve calendrical animals with the ten heavenly stems) and the practice of identifying one's age by the calendrical animal of one's year of birth are still popular today.

THREE LARGE PAINTED
POTTERY FIGURES OF ARISTOCRATIC WOMEN

Tang dynasty

Height 73 cm (28.4 in)

Excavated in 1986 in Hansenzhai in
the city of Xian, Shaanxi

Bureau of Cultural Relics And Gardening
of Xian, Shaanxi

These three female figurines, excavated from the same site, have ample faces, delicate eyes and eyebrows, and small, red-lipped mouths. Each wears a different facial expression and hairstyle. Their figures are full, displaying an ideal of feminine beauty and dignity thought to have been made popular in the early Tang period by Yang Guifei, the imperial consort of Emperor Xuanzong (r. 712–756). They have been exquisitely sculpted and are highly realistic. These figurines are a rare source of information about the sculpture and styles of the Tang dynasty.

ANIMAL TOMB GUARDIAN IN THREE-COLORED GLAZE

Tang dynasty

Height 103.5 cm (40.3 in)

Excavated in 1981 from the tomb of An Pu and his wife at Dongshan, Lungmen, in the city of Loyang, Henan

Cultural Relics Excavation Team of Loyang, Henan

Three-color ceramic figurines are among the most famous Tang dynasty artifacts. Animal tomb guardians, such as this strange beast with a human face and an animal body, were placed in tombs to protect against evil forces and grave robbers. The figure is covered with a lead glaze to which various minerals were added to create vibrant colors. On his head are a tall spear and long horns. His top-knot is swirled like a conch, and two long animal ears flare from the sides. Spiked wings sprout from his ribs, and his feet are cloven hooves. Seated on a square stand, his appearance is fierce and imposing with an air of mystery.

The tomb of An Pu in Loyang, the eastern capital of the Tang dynasty, was never robbed. Figurines such as this animal guardian are among the finest found in the region.

HEAVENLY KING (DEVA) IN THREE-COLORED GLAZE

Tang dynasty

Height 113 cm (44 in)

Excavated from Guanlin
in the city of Loyang, Henan

Loyang Museum, Henan

This supernatural figure wears a crown and armor on his body with right and left protruding breast protectors. On both shoulders are open-mouthed animal heads and below he wears knee protectors and pointed shoes. He stands on an ox, the left foot on the ox's head and the right on its body, symbolizing the unchallenged spiritual majesty of a heavenly king protecting the occupant of the tomb.

FIGURE OF A CIVIL OFFICIAL IN THREE-COLORED GLAZE

Tang dynasty

Height 107 cm (41.7 in)

Excavated from Guanlin in the city of Loyang, Henan

Loyang Museum, Henan

This figure wears a long gown under an outer jacket. On the upper portion of his body is a belt and he wears flat-toed shoes. The hat in the shape of a mountain is rare. His hands are folded across his chest, and his facial expression is thoughtful, projecting the dignity and intelligence of an official of the Tang court.

LARGE PAINTED POTTERY HORSE

Tang dynasty

Height 87 cm (33.9); length 93 cm (36.2 in)

Excavated in Loyang, Henan

Henan Provincial Museum

The Chinese have always loved horses. Military men loved them because they were companions on the battlefield; the literati loved them because they liked to compare themselves to the "special breed that can run a thousand miles." This literary convention was particularly strong during the Han and Tang dynasties.

  Pottery horses are funerary objects frequently found in Tang tombs. This large, painted pottery horse has its head lowered and its mouth opened while neighing. Its body is covered with a white glaze. The saddle is covered with red brocade and on the leather straps decorations are hung in the shape of peaches with carved green toads. This splendid embellishment reflects the Tang people's love of horses. The horses they rode had their tails tied with ribbons and the saddle flaps had protectors against mud. The peach-shaped decorations on the straps were alluded to in a line from a Tang poem: "apricot leaves garnish the purple reins." The toad is a guardian against evil.

CAMEL IN THREE-COLORED GLAZE

Tang dynasty

Height 81 cm (31.5 in); length 68 cm (26.5 in)

Excavated in 1973 at Guanlin in the city of Loyang, Henan

Cultural Relics Excavation Team of Loyang, Henan

The frequent subject of camels in Tang dynasty sculpture reflects the importance of the Silk Road. Camels were the main form of transport along the Silk Road because they could carry goods, move rapidly, and endure suffering and hardship, and they were well adapted to the difficulties of the desert environment. This camel stands erect with raised head and has a carrying bag on his back. He is represented with great vitality as he raises his neck and cries out, his four hooves staggered, presenting an image of the "ship of the desert" treading the Silk Road.

SILVER BOWL WITH DESIGN OF DEER
AND DIVINE FUNGUS (*LINGZHI*)

Tang dynasty

Height 10 cm (3.9 in); diameter 50 cm (19.5 in);
width of rim 7 cm (2.7 in); weight 2200 g (77.6 oz)

Excavated from Dayegu village
in Kuancheng district, Hebei

Kuancheng District Museum, Hebei

The edge of this silver bowl has been worked in the shape of six caltrop flower petals. On each petal is a repoussé (raised) cluster of pomegranate flowers. In the center of the bowl is a repoussé deer bearing on its head a divine fungus believed to grant immortality. The deer's head is raised and its tail curves upward. On its body are spots like plum blossoms. The dish rests on three legs in the shape of curling leaves.

Tang silver and gold ware is renowned for its intricate decoration and craftsmanship. It is also rare, since these objects were often the first to be taken when a tomb was looted. This silver bowl belongs to the high Tang period (eighth century). Techniques such as repoussé came to China by way of Persia early in the Tang era, allowing for great aesthetic improvements over earlier bronze casting methods.

Among the hundreds of gold and silver artifacts unearthed at Hejia village in the southern suburb of Xian in October 1970 are two octagonal gilt cups decorated with musicians and dancers. Each cup has eight faces adorned with figures of foreign entertainers holding musical instruments. The handle of this cup, one of the two, is decorated with the heads of two foreigners looking in opposite directions. A string of beads frames each facet and the base is decorated with interlocking honeysuckle scrolls. This exquisitely made cup in the Persian style, once used as a wine cup by the imperial family of the Tang dynasty, provides good evidence of cultural exchange between China and other countries of the world.

OCTAGONAL GOLD CUP DECORATED WITH ENTERTAINERS

Tang dynasty

Height 6.3 cm (2.4 in)
Diameter of mouth 6 cm (2.3 in)

Excavated in 1970 at Hejiacun in the city of Xian, Shaanxi

The Historical Museum of Shaanxi

GOLD HEATER (*CHENG*) WITH PAIR OF LIONS AND FLOWER DESIGNS

Tang dynasty

Height 3.2 cm (1.2 in); diameter 9 cm (3.5 in)

Excavated in 1970 at Hejiacun in the city of Xian, Shaanxi

The Historical Museum of Shaanxi

A *cheng* is an ancient vessel for heating. Many silver heaters have been excavated but gold ones are extremely rare. This gold tureen has a shallow belly, three feet in the shape of animals, and a short handle. The outside surface of the vessel has raised decorations of nine radiating leaf veins interspersed with pearls, a pair of birds carrying ribbons, another pair of birds holding a talisman, a lion, and flowers. The bottom of the vessel is decorated with a pair of repoussé lions. The form is elegant and the carving is delicate with harmonious designs. It is one of the great treasures of Tang gold and silver ware.

SILVER BOWL WITH DESIGN OF A PAIR OF LIONS

Tang dynasty

Height 3.5 cm (1.3 in)
Diameter 12.5 cm (4.8 in)

Excavated in 1970 at Hejiacun
in the city of Xian, Shaanxi

The Historical Museum of Shaanxi

Silver bowls were practical objects used by the
Tang aristocracy. The sides of this one have been
engraved with a design of pomegranates. Ringing
the bottom of the bowl is a pattern of curled
leaves like waves. In the center is a pair of lions.
Their front legs are lifted, their tails are raised,
and they hold branches of intertwined flowers in
their mouths. The open space beneath their feet is
filled with flower branches. The composition of
these designs is well balanced, demonstrating the
highly polished technique of gold and silver vessel
decoration during the Tang.

GILT SILVER BOWL WITH DESIGN OF DIVINE ANIMALS

Tang dynasty

Height 3.2 cm (1.2 in)
Diameter 11 cm (4.3 in)

Excavated in 1970 at Hejiacun
in the city of Xian, Shaanxi

The Historical Museum of Shaanxi

The bottom of this silver bowl is a gilded,
repoussé image of sea creatures. The walls have a
pattern of fourteen lines representing waves while
the lip is shaped like flower petals. The design of
this bowl shows an ingenious imagination. When
filled with water or wine, it seems as if the ocean-
dwelling animals are playing among the waves.

SILVER THREE-TIERED CENSER WITH FIVE FEET AND PIERCED CLOUD DESIGN

Tang dynasty

Height 31.5 cm (12.2 in)
Diameter of mouth 16 cm (6.2 in)
Weight 3995 g (141 oz)

Excavated in 1970 at Hejiacun in the city of Xian, Shaanxi

The Historical Museum of Shaanxi

Perfume was not widely used in ancient China. Instead, incense was burned, creating a need for many kinds of censers. This particular censer consists of three sections: a pan, a cover, and a lid. The lowest tier is the pan with five legs, between which hang five chains, one of which is missing. Resting on the pan is the cover, held in place by three protruding cloud decorations raised above the lip of the pan. Both the cover and the lid contain pierced cloud designs in the "*ruyi*" motif, which means, "May your wishes come true." These openings allow the fragrance of the incense to disperse. On the bottom of the pan is an inked inscription in five ideographs, "Three-tiers holding five-and-a-half *jin*." Inscriptions indicating the number of parts and the total amount they contain are often found on gold and silver vessels in China to discourage the theft of individual parts.

RELIQUARY SET IN FOUR PIECES
WITH GOLD INNER COFFIN
AND SILVER OUTER COFFIN

Tang dynasty

Excavated in 1964 from the foundation of a pagoda in
the Tang dynasty Temple of the Great Clouds (Dayunsi)
in Jingchuan district, Gansu

Gansu Provincial Museum

1. GILT BRONZE CONTAINER
   Length 12.3 cm (4.8 in); width 12.3 cm (4.8 in);
   height 13.2 cm (5.1 in); weight 590 g (20.8 oz)

2. SILVER OUTER COFFIN
   Length 8.4 cm (3.2 in); width 8.4 cm (3.2 in);
   height 9.3 cm (3.6 in); weight 350 g (12.3 oz)

3. GOLD INNER COFFIN
   Length 7.5 cm (2.9 in); width 5.4 cm (2.1 in);
   height 6 cm (2.3 in); weight 110 g (3.8 oz)

4. RELIQUARY BOTTLE WITH RELIC
   OF FOURTEEN GRAINS
   Diameter of body 2.1 cm (0.82 in);
   diameter of mouth 0.5 cm (0.2 in);
   height 2.6 cm (1 in)

This reliquary set with coffins was excavated from
the underground burial chamber of a pagoda
among the ruins of the Tang dynasty Temple
of the Great Clouds. The gilt bronze container
was originally placed in a stone reliquary box on
the cover of which was the inscription, in sixteen
clerical-style ideographs, "Reliquary Box of the
Temple of the Great Clouds in Jingchuan of the
Great Zhou dynasty Containing Fourteen Grains."
The sides were carved with intertwining branches
of Central Asian lotuses and also bore an
inscription in more than one thousand ideographs
bearing the names of the benefactors. The bronze
container is nearly square in shape with a lid like

an inverted dipper inlaid with a twelve-petal lotus
blossom in silver. In the center is an inlaid silver
pearl in the shape of a peach. At the back of the
lid are two silver hinges. On the front is a silver
hinge in the shape of a five-petal flower and two
silver catches in the shape of six-petal flowers.
These hold a lock of gold and silver with a
matching key. The entire body of the container is
gilded and covered with a pattern of honeysuckle
flowers against a ground of pearls.

The silver outer coffin was found placed
within the gilt bronze container. The top is like an
inverted roof tile. Two rings are attached on both
sides. Its base is trapezoidal with the front wider

than the back. There are railings on all four sides decorated with caltrop forms. The silver outer coffin is decorated with opposing patterns of honeysuckle against a ground of pearls.

The gold inner coffin was found placed inside the silver outer coffin and is similar in shape. The centers of the top and sides are inlaid with pearls. Gold lotus petals are inlaid with turquoise, quartz, and other materials. A six-petal lotus blossom decorated with lotus sepals and inlaid quartz has been applied to the center of the back.

The glass reliquary bottle was found placed inside the gold inner coffin. It is white and translucent with a long neck, round middle, and flat bottom. The relic—fourteen grains shaped like kernels of rice with the consistency of pearls, through which tiny holes have been drilled—was found placed inside the bottle. The largest grain is barely 0.5 mm in length, and the smallest is 0.01 mm.

These relics are believed to be the ashes of the Sakyamuni Buddha (ca. 565–486 B.C.). According to Buddhist tradition, after the Buddha died and was cremated, his body was transformed into relics the size of rice kernels which could not be pulverized or scorched and sometimes produced brilliant light and divine effects. A further legend states that the ancient Indian King Asoka (r. 268–232 B.C.) placed these relics in 84,000 containers and distributed them throughout the world in order to spread Buddhism. A Buddhist sutra states, "If there is no genuine relic, then a relic can still be created out of gold, silver, glazed tile, crystal, jasper, glass, and other valuable materials," so that even sand, herbs, or pieces of bamboo or wood can serve as relics. The relic in this exhibition seems to have been made from pearl or something similar.

Based on the inscription on the stone box and reasoning from historical records, in the first year of the *yanshou* era of the Sui emperor Wen (A.D. 601), the holy relics were distributed to thirty prefectures throughout the country and reliquary pagodas were built to house them. This reliquary bottle was probably placed in the reliquary pagoda at the Temple of National Prosperity (Daxingguosi) in Jing prefecture at that time. Later, the pagoda fell into disrepair. During the time of Wu Zitian (Empress Wu, r. 684–704), this temple was reconstructed as the Temple of the Great Clouds. The reliquary bottle and stone box were recovered from beneath the pagoda, and a newly created gold inner coffin, silver outer coffin, gilt bronze container, and stone box were reburied in the vault of the pagoda in the first year of the *yanzai* era (A.D. 649).

This reliquary set is intricately manufactured and splendidly decorated. It is a valuable source for studying the history of Buddhism during the Sui and Tang dynasties as well as the history of handicrafts.

Relics from the
Tomb of the Princess of Chen
from the Kingdom of Liao (907–1125)

The kingdom of Liao (907–1125) was a local regime established by the Qidan, a minority tribe in the north. The discovery in July 1985 of the joint tomb of the princess of Liao and her husband, a commandant-escort, in Naiman Banner, Inner Mongolia, was an extremely important find in the archaeological history of the Liao dynasty. An epitaph engraved in stone discovered in the tomb tells us clearly that this tomb was constructed in the seventh year of the *kaitai* era of the Liao emperor Shengzong (1081). The occupants of the tomb were the granddaughter of Empress Dowager Xiao, who was also known as the Empress Dowager of Heavenly Obedience, and her husband, Xiao Shaoju, commandant-escort and acting grand preceptor to the military commissioner of Taining. She was also the niece of Yelü Longxu, the Liao emperor Shengzong (r. 982–1054). The princess died at the age of eighteen, and her husband died at thirty-five.

The tomb is composed of many rooms lined in brick. It was built 13 feet in depth and 52.4 feet in length, and consists of a passageway, a courtyard, a gate, a front chamber, two side chambers on the east and west, and a rear chamber. The occupants were placed on a base in the rear chamber dressed from head to toe in the unique burial clothes and gold-and-silver ornaments of the Qidan aristocracy. On their heads they wore crowns gilded with silver and gold. Their faces were covered with dazzling lifelike masks made of thin gold sheets which had been hammered and then assembled. Their heads rested on pillows decorated in patterns of gold and silver. Over undergarments and under their jackets they were wrapped in wire mesh woven with silver thread and linked with silver belts. Their shoes were silver with gold flower designs. They wore amber-and-pearl pendant earrings, and ornaments of white jade hung from their belts.

These funerary outfits demonstrate the increasing assimilation of Han Chinese culture by the Qidan, who originated in the northern grassland steppe. The Qidan had already abandoned the simpler burial customs of their earlier period and appropriated the Han fashion of lavish burials. But regardless of how extravagantly gold and silver were used to enclose the bodies, they could not be eternally preserved. All that remained of the bodies of the princess and commandant-escort were teeth and portions of the skulls; the rest had long since turned to dust.

Two sets of equestrian objects placed in the western side-chamber, built to resemble the stable of the tomb occupants, still reflect the customs of people of the grasslands. The bridles, reins, ropes, saddles, saddle blankets, halters, and cruppers are all made of silver. Attached to the saddles and cruppers are dozens of white jade ornaments carved in the shapes of animals. The saddle blankets are engraved and painted with facing dragons, phoenixes, and floating clouds. These two sets of equestrian objects are not the kind used every day but were specially manufactured for burial.

GOLD MASK

Liao dynasty (907–1125)

Length 20.5 cm (8 in); width 17.2 cm (6.7 in)
Weight 184 g (6.5 oz)

Excavated in 1986 from the tomb
of the Princess of Chen
in Naiman District, Zhelimu Prefecture,
Inner Mongolia Autonomous Region

Inner Mongolia Institute for Archaeology
and Cultural Relics

This mask was placed over the face of the Princess of Chen and has been worked in semi-repoussé. It displays an attitude of peacefulness and solemn dignity. Thirty-three small holes around the edge were used to attach it to a silver wire mesh which held it to the head. Burial masks of gold and silver were a unique custom of the Qidan people and were recorded in texts of that time. Many gilt bronze masks have been recovered from excavations in the past but this mask of solid gold attests to the high rank of the princess and the commandant-escort.

SILVER MESH BURIAL SUIT

Liao dynasty

Length 175 cm (68.2 in)

Excavated in 1986 from the tomb
of the Princess of Chen
in Naiman District, Zhelimu Prefecture,
Inner Mongolia Autonomous Region

Inner Mongolia Institute for Archaeology
and Cultural Relics

This is one of two special funerary suits woven
of silver wire. Tailored for the bodies of the
princess and the commandant-escort, the burial
suits consist of seven large pieces, one each for the
head, arms, hands, chest and back, abdomen, legs,
and feet. After each piece was completed, it was
placed over the undergarments and then sewn
together to form a complete burial suit.
Outergarments were placed over the suit,
including a belt, a mask, silver shoes, and jewelry.
Based on analysis, the silver wire is 91.77% pure
with 2.48% bronze and 5.75% other materials.

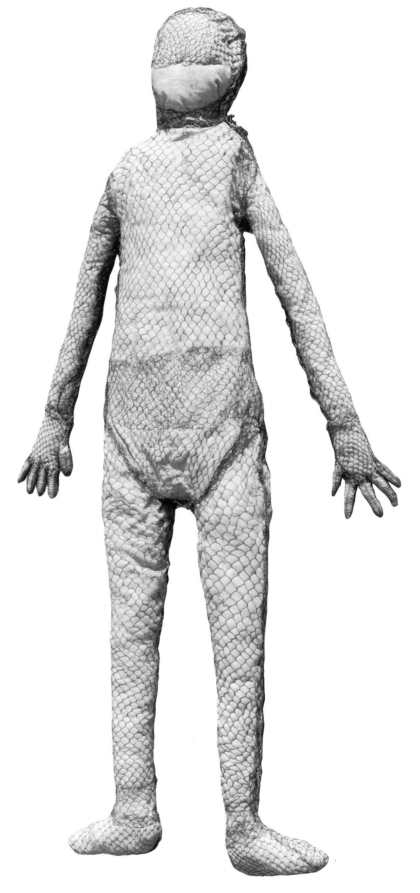

Relics from the
Dingling Tomb of the Wanli Emperor and Imperial Household
from the Ming Dynasty (1368–1644)

The Dingling Tomb is located at the foot of Tianshou Mountain in the north of Changping district in the city of Beijing. Thirteen emperors of the Ming dynasty are buried here, beginning with the Yongle emperor (r. 1403–1424), who moved the capital to Beijing. The area of the tomb is built into the mountain and surrounded by it on the east, north, and west. The tombs were built in sequence as follows: Deling, Yongling, Jingling, Changling, Xianling, Qingling, Yuling, Maoling, Tailing, Kangling, Dingling, Zhaoling, and Siling. A wall surrounds the tomb area. On the south side is a large palace-style gate to the left and right of which is a pillar with a notice ordering everyone to dismount. On each side of the gate the symbolic Tiger and Dragon mountains symbolize the geomantic placement of the gate in relation to the tombs. The 1155-yard-long Sacred Way leads from the gate northward.

On both sides of the Sacred Way are thirty-six stone memorial pillars, animals, and human figures, among which are lions, camels, mythical *qilin*, and military and civil officials.

Thirteen emperors are buried at the site of the Ming tombs. The Dingling tomb of the Wanli emperor is the only one excavated to date.

Beyond the Sacred Way is the Dragon and Phoenix Gate through which one arrives at the Changling Tomb in the heart of the tomb area. This is the grave of the Yongle emperor, the first to be buried here. Everything strictly follows the rules of Chinese *fengshui* geomancy—a kind of divination by means of figures or lines formed by points on the earth—in its careful arrangement and ingenious conception.

The Dingling Tomb is the grave of Zhu Yijun, the Ming emperor Shenzong, also known as the Wanli emperor (r. 1572–1620), together with Empress Xiaoduan (the emperor's first wife) and Empress Xiaojing. Empress Xiaojing was a royal concubine, mother of the emperor's first son, and grandmother of Emperor Xizong, also known as the Tianqi emperor (r. 1620–1627). Zhu Yijun (1563–1620) was the thirteenth Ming emperor. He ascended the throne at age nine and reigned for forty-eight years, the longest of any Ming emperor. He was given the posthumous title "Glorious Emperor, Model of Heaven, in Accord with the Way, Perspicacious, Dignified, Austere, Brilliant in Culture and Meritorious in War, Peaceful, Benevolent and

Supremely Filial." His temple name was "Shenzong" (Divine Ancestor).

The Wanli emperor, like other emperors before him, personally chose the site of his tomb and set its architectural dimensions. Construction was begun in the twelfth year of the Wanli era (1584) and took eighteen years to complete, costing approximately 80,000 ounces of silver. This was equivalent to the income of the national treasury for two years.

The Dingling Tomb consists of stone steles in front, two paths with gates leading to the palace-style wall, the Sacrificial Hall, the Gate of the Ling Star behind the hall, the Soul Tower, and the "City Wall and Dome." The Gate of the Ling Star divides the human world from the world of the dead. In between the Gate of the Ling Star and the Soul Tower is a huge stone table. The Soul Tower is the highest building in the tomb and marks the grave. Beneath the "City Wall and Dome" is the "underground palace" or mausoleum.

The underground palace consists of a front chamber, a middle chamber with two side chambers, and a rear chamber. The underground palace together with its tunnel is 286 feet long

The Sacred Way is lined with eighteen pairs of mythical creatures, human figures, and animals, each carved from a single piece of marble.

and 155 feet wide with a total area of 12,858 square feet. In the middle chamber are three sacred thrones for the Wanli emperor and his two empresses. In front of each of the thrones were five yellow-glazed ritual objects: an incense censer, two candleholders, and two flower vases. In front of these five objects was an eternal lamp made of blue and white porcelain.

The rear chamber is where the coffins of the emperor and empresses were placed and is the main portion of the underground palace. It is taller and larger than the front and middle chambers. The bases for the coffins were located slightly to the west of the center of the chamber. In the middle was the Wanli emperor and to the left and right were the Empresses Xiaoduan and Xiaojing, respectively.

Altogether, 2,648 funerary objects were excavated from the tomb. The crown with three dragons and six phoenixes in this exhibition belonged to the Empress Xiaojing. The other objects, made predominantly of jade and porcelain, reflect those in daily use by the imperial family and aristocrats during the Ming dynasty.

CROWN WITH THREE DRAGONS AND
TWO PHOENIXES OF THE
WANLI EMPEROR'S EMPRESS XIAOJING

Height 35.5 cm (13.8 in)
Diameter 20 cm (7.8 in)
Weight 2,905 g (102.5 oz)

Excavated in 1958 from the Dingling Tomb of the
Ming dynasty in Changping district, Beijing

Palace Museum, Beijing

The most magnificent ornamental headdress for women in ancient China, the phoenix crown, was worn as part of ceremonial dress by empresses and imperial concubines at their investiture, when visiting temples, and at court occasions. During the early Ming dynasty, regulations governing the design of the crown were quite strict, but by the late Ming period these specifications were relaxed.

Worn by the Empress Xiaojing, this phoenix crown was excavated in 1958 from the Dingling Tomb of the Ming dynasty in Changping district, Beijing. Its frame was constructed of slender bamboo strips that were then lacquered. The body was inlaid with ninety-five precious stones and embellished with flat clouds in the *ruyi* motif with an appliqué of kingfisher feathers. On the front and on the left and right sides of the crown are three dragons in twisted gold wire. Their heads point down and they hold strands of pearls in their mouths. In the lower rear of the crown, on both the left and right sides, are three side pieces on which are engraved dragons, phoenixes, clouds, and flowers with a kingfisher feather appliqué.

Empress Xiaojing was from the Wang family and began as a palace maiden to the empress dowager, Xiaoduan, in the Cining Palace. In June 1582 she became Concubine Gong, since she had become pregnant by the emperor. In August, she gave birth to their eldest son, Zhu Changluo. Upon her death, shortly before the death of the emperor, she was buried in her own tomb, separate from the one the emperor had prepared for himself, since according to Ming dynasty regulations, only empresses could be buried in the imperial tombs. In August, 1620, Zhu Yijun, the Wanli emperor, died. The eldest son, Zhu Changluo, succeeded to the throne, and was considering the proper posthumous title for his mother when he suddenly died. The grandson Zhu Youjiao succeeded him and bestowed the title "Kind, Virtuous, Respectful, Chaste, Charitable, of the Divine Succession, Sagely, Empress-Dowager Xiaojing." In this way, she could be buried in the Dingling Tomb.

BELT OF TWENTY LIGHT GREEN JADE PLAQUES WITH PIERCED DESIGN OF CLOUDS AND DRAGONS

Ten rectangular plaques:
Length 6.7–11.8 cm (2.6–4.6 in)
Width 5.2–5.4 cm (2–2.1 in)

Six peach-shaped plaques:
Length 5.1 cm (1.9 in)

Four thin rectangular plaques:
Length 2.1 cm (0.8 in)
Width 5.1 cm (1.9 in)

Palace Museum, Beijing

The weighted end piece, rectangular, and peach-shaped plaques are all carved in pierced designs of a dragon with divine fungus and flowers. One of the rectangular plaques—carved in a pierced design of a dragon among flowers—differs from the others and was probably fashioned later. The thin, rectangular plaques are also carved in a pierced design.

**GREEN JADE WATER HOLDER
CARVED IN THE SHAPE OF
AN AUSPICIOUS ANIMAL**

Height 5.9 cm (2.3 in)
Diameter 1.7 cm (0.6 in)

Palace Museum, Beijing

This water holder is made of green jade carved
in the shape of an auspicious animal. A round
reservoir for water is carved into its back. A
stopper carved in the shape of an animal fits into
a hole in the top. When used, water was poured
through the mouth onto an inkstone for grinding
ink. The water holder was an object used in the
scholar's studio. The literati painted or practiced
calligraphy in their studios and often employed
writing implements and decorative objects made
of jade.

**GREEN JADE SQUARE BOX
WITH ENGRAVED DESIGN OF
LANDSCAPE AND PAVILIONS**

Height 4.8 cm (1.8 in)
Diameter 6.8 cm (2.6 in)

Palace Museum, Beijing

This square box is made of green jade with a
slightly arched cover. A picture of a landscape
consisting of mountains, trees, pavilions, and
boats on a river has been lightly engraved on top.
The edges of the cover and box are engraved in a
meander pattern. The bottom rests on a square
foot. During the middle and late Ming periods,
jade crafts were influenced by literati painting. All
manner of mountains and trees, figures, animals,
birds, and winding streams were clearly depicted
in jade, revealing the charm of the paintings of
these periods.

GREEN JADE OCTAGONAL CUP WITH A PAIR OF CARVED COILED DRAGON HANDLES

Height of cup 5.8 cm (2.2 in)
Diameter of mouth 6.3 cm (2.4 in)

Height of tray 0.8 cm (0.3 in)
Length 23.8 cm (9.2 in); width 16.3 cm (6.3 in)

Palace Museum, Beijing

This lustrous octagonal cup of green jade with mottled black markings is flawless. It was used for drinking wine during the Jiajing period and could also serve as a purely decorative object. The outer edge is engraved with a meander pattern. On both sides are handles in the shape of pierced carvings of a dragon with a coiled *kui* dragon. The front claws of both dragons grasp the lip of the cup so that they look at each other with open mouths while their tails are attached to the middle of the cup. The jade tray is shaped like a crabapple blossom with an octagonal center to hold the cup. Two ascending dragons are carved on the surface of the tray and its edge is engraved with intertwined leaves. The engraving is intricate, revealing powerful, broad strokes.

GREEN JADE BRUSH WASHER IN THE SHAPE OF A CRABAPPLE BLOSSOM WITH THREE HORNLESS DRAGONS CARVED IN RELIEF

Height 6 cm (2.3 in)
Diameter lengthwise 7.3 cm (2.8 in)
Diameter at width 5.7 cm (2.2 in)

Palace Museum, Beijing

This brush washer is intricately carved of green jade in the shape of a crabapple blossom. The body is lightly engraved with crabapple blossoms. Protruding from it are three coiled, hornless dragons resting on the blossoms. Their form is striking and lively. This style of brush washer is often found among scholarly objects used in the Ming dynasty palace.

LONG-NECKED PORCELAIN VASE FROM THE WANLI ERA WITH MULTICOLORED DECORATION OF EGRETS AND LOTUSES

Height 44.5 cm (17.3 in)
Diameter at mouth 7.5 cm (2.9 in)

Palace Museum, Beijing

The mouth of this vase is shaped like a head of garlic, giving it the name "garlic head vase." The body is covered with a white glaze on which multicolored decorations have been painted. Around the belly of the vase is a design of mandarin ducks among lotuses, along with willows, sparrows, and egrets. The atmosphere of the entire scene is highly animated. In addition to the blue and white designs, the white glaze background has been painted with brown or black outlines which were then filled in with rich colors such as red, green, yellow, and purple. This vase is a product of the highest period in the development of Ming dynasty multicolored porcelain.

PORCELAIN BOX FROM THE WANLI ERA
IN BLUE AND WHITE GLAZE WITH
DESIGN OF DRAGONS AMONG BRANCHES

Height 10.5 cm (4 in)
Diameter at mouth 16.3 cm (6.3 in)

Palace Museum, Beijing

The cover of this round box is slightly arched and inside are seven compartments shaped like flower petals with an inscription on the bottom that reads, "Made during the Wanli era of the Great Ming Dynasty" in six regular-style ideographs.

This box was used to hold food. It is entirely decorated in blue and white glaze with a principal design on both cover and body of dragons among flowers. The cover also contains a design of lotus blossoms and water ripples in four sections that are clearly articulated and well arranged. There are many piercings in the cover that allow the aroma of the contents to escape and also serve a decorative function. This is a classic example of blue and white porcelain ware from the Wanli era.

GILDED PAGODA ON STONE BASE

Height 51 cm (19.9 in)
Width 38 cm (14.8 in)
Weight 62 kg (136.7 lb)

Excavated in 1956 from the underground vault
of the pagoda at the Temple of Vast Awakening
(Hungjuesi) on Niushou Mountain in the city of
Nanjing, Jiangsu

Nanjing Museum

1. Gilded Lamaist Pagoda
   Height 34 cm (12.2 in)

2. Red Stone Base Representing Mt. Sumeru
   Width 38 cm (14.8 in)

3. Four Blue and White Porcelain Covered Jars

   First and Second Jars:
   Diameter at mouth 7.2 cm (2.8 in)
   Height 14.5 cm (5.6 in)

   Third and Fourth Jars:
   Diameter at mouth 6 cm (2.3 in)
   Height 14 cm (5.4 in)

4. Gilt Bronze Nirvana Figurine
   Length 8.8 cm (3.4 in)
   Width 3.8 cm (1.5 in)
   Height 5 cm (1.9 in)

5. Gilt Bronze Inner Coffin
   Length 10.4 cm (4 in)
   Width 5.2 cm (2 in)
   Height 5.5 cm (2.1)

6. Lead Outer Coffin
   Length 11.2 cm (4.3 in)
   Width 6.3 cm (2.4 in)
   Height 6.5 cm (2.5 in)

This reliquary, in the shape of a Lamaist pagoda, was used in Buddhist ceremonies. It has four entrances. The interior of the pagoda contains an altar which is a mandala, as well as images of the Sakyamuni Buddha and the Vedas guardians. The top is decorated with symbols of the Wheel of Existence, the thirteen heavens, a parasol, and pearls. The base of the pagoda is divided into three levels which fit into a carved stone base representing Mount Sumeru. Half-kneeling guardians are carved in relief into the front face of the base. The right face is carved with lions playing with pearls, the left face with a pair of deer about to lock horns, and the rear with

dragons among clouds. The blue and white jar placed at each of the four corners of the stone base contained fragrant medicinal herbs. On a small flat terrace on the front face of the stone platform is a gilded reclining Buddha representing the Mahaparinirvana, or Death of the Buddha. There are also gilt bronze inner and outer coffins.

On the lowest level of the base of the pagoda is an inscription, "Presented for the Eternal Use of the Temple of Vast Awakening on Niushou Mountain in Jinling. Donated by the Buddhist Disciple and Imperial Eunuch Li Fushan." This reflects the spiritual life of the aristocracy at this time and their faith in Buddhism.

Decorative Objects and Fashions from the
Imperial Palaces of the Qing Dynasty (1644–1911)

Shenyang, called "Shengjing" (Divine Capital) during the Qing dynasty, was the last capital built by the Qing rulers outside the Great Wall before they conquered the Central Plains area of China. The city walls of Shengjing are formal and majestic, and the imperial palace is painted in a variety of colors, giving it an awe-inspiring appearance. By the end of the fourth decade of the Qianlong emperor's reign (r. 1735–1795), the original imperial palace in Shengjing had been expanded into a series of palaces in conformity with proper imperial proportions and style. This was intended to further demonstrate the magnificence of the imperial family.

The imperial palace in Shenyang was largely completed in its present form by the end of the eighteenth century. These decorative objects and clothes from the Shenyang palace symbolize the absolutely supreme position of the emperor. Wherever the Qing emperor held court in the palace, elaborately carved screens and a throne were set up. On both sides of this, a mass of objects such as figures of elephants symbolic of peace, candleholders, incense censers, and auspicious *luduan* animals created an atmosphere of majesty and solemn dignity. When a great ceremony was carried out, the emperor wore a dragon robe, and racks of bells and chimes were set up in the hall to play ritual music for the occasion. Flags and banners, parasols, awnings, symbolic axes, and a spear in the shape of a vertical hand were arrayed before the hall and referred to collectively as the "honor guard." Their function was to symbolize the grave importance of the ceremony and the awesome dignity of the emperor. Whenever the emperor set forth, these would precede him as yet another manifestation of his high and noble position.

Most of these objects were created during the Qianlong era (1736–1795). They are technically superb and decorated with classic elegance and beauty. The colors yellow and gold predominate, and the main motifs are the dragon, phoenix, immortal cranes, plants, and flowers, which, according to Chinese tradition, all allude to wealth, nobility, and auspiciousness. These rare cultural relics can provide a general understanding of the ceremonies of the Qing dynasty palace and handicraft techniques.

**GOLD-LACQUER SCREEN
WITH SEVEN LEAVES AND DESIGN OF
DRAGONS AMONG CLOUDS**

Height 408 cm (159.1 in)
Width 424 cm (165.3 in)

Shenyang Palace Museum

Decorated with elaborately carved gold-lacquer
dragons in the Qianlong era, this seven-panel
screen was placed behind the imperial throne.

GOLD-LACQUER THRONE ENSEMBLE
IN SIX PIECES WITH PIERCED DESIGNS
OF DRAGONS AMONG CLOUDS

Height 186 cm (72.5 in); length 180 cm (70.2 in);
width 165 cm (64.3 in)

Shenyang Palace Museum

Also from the Qianlong era, this seat was placed
in the principal hall of the palace and used when
the emperor held court in order to conduct affairs
of state and receive formal congratulations.

**CARVED RED-LACQUER
SPITTOON INLAID WITH JADE**

Height 7.5 cm (2.9 in)
Diameter 14.8 cm (5.7 in)

Shenyang Palace Museum

This carved red-lacquer spittoon was placed next
to the emperor's seat to be used whenever he felt
like expectorating.

WHITE JADE *RUYI* SCEPTER

Length 42 cm (16.3 in)
Width 9.8 cm (3.8 in)
Thickness 5.5 cm (2.1 in)

Shenyang Palace Museum

This was made during the Qianlong era. Scepters
such as these were used by rulers and officials
during the Qing dynasty as gifts on festive
occasions to symbolize good fortune and the
granting of wishes.

PAIR OF BRIGHT YELLOW SATIN HAND RESTS WITH MULTICOLORED EMBROIDERY

17 x 22 x 22 cm (6.6 x 8.5 x 8.5 in)

Shenyang Palace Museum

These hand rests, made in the Qianlong era, are part of a set with the cushion below, and were placed on the emperor's throne.

BRIGHT YELLOW SATIN CUSHION WITH MULTICOLORED EMBROIDERY

54 x 99 cm (21 x 38.6 in)

Shenyang Palace Museum

This Qianlong era cushion was used by the emperor when he sat on the throne or on couches.

**PAIR OF GOLD-LACQUER
ROUND STANDS**

Height 89.5 cm (34.9 in)
Diameter of surface 49 cm (19.1 in)

Shenyang Palace Museum

These Qianlong era round stands were used in the palace for the display of decorative objects.

PAIR OF CLOISONNÉ ELEPHANTS
SYMBOLIZING PEACE

Height 41 cm (15.9 in)
Length 22 cm (8.5 in)
Width 10 cm (3.9 in)

Shenyang Palace Museum

These Qianlong era cloisonné elephants were
typically placed near the throne. In ancient China,
elephants were regarded as auspicious animals.
These elephants carry vases on their backs and
allude to the hope of peace throughout the world.

PAIR OF CLOISONNÉ *LUDUAN* ANIMALS

Height 37 cm (14.4 in)
Length 26.5 cm (10.3 in)
Width 23 cm (8.9 in)

Shenyang Palace Museum

Luduan were strange, legendary animals capable of
distinguishing between good and evil. They were
placed beside the throne to symbolize that the
emperor protected by the animals was a virtuous
and intelligent ruler.

PAIR OF CLOISONNÉ CANDLEHOLDERS
IN THE FORM OF CRANES

Height 149 cm (58.1 in)
Height of stand 39 cm (15.2 in)
Diameter 31 cm (12 in)

Shenyang Palace Museum

These Qianlong era candleholders in the form of
cranes were placed before the throne and
symbolized auspiciousness and longevity in
ancient China.

**PAIR OF RED-LACQUER STANDS
PAINTED IN GOLD**

Height 51 cm (19.8 in)
Diameter 56.3 cm (21.9 in)

Shenyang Palace Museum

These Qianlong era stands were used in the palace
for the display of decorative objects.

**PAIR OF LARGE
CLOISONNÉ INCENSE CENSERS
IN THE FORM OF PAGODAS**

Height 117 cm (45.6 in)
Diameter of base 22 cm (8.5 in)

Shenyang Palace Museum

Also placed near the throne, these tall incense
censers in the form of pagodas burned
sandalwood incense.

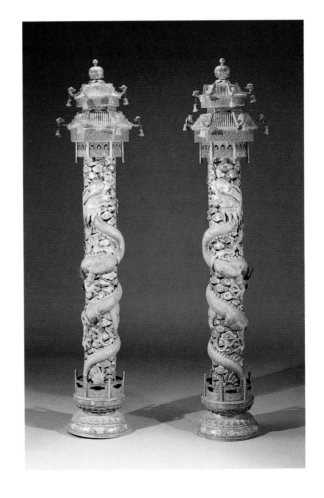

PAIR OF LARGE CLOISONNÉ INCENSE CENSERS

Height 120 cm (46.8 in)
Diameter 86.5 cm (33.7 in)

Shenyang Palace Museum

These cloisonné incense censers were placed in
front of the throne for burning coal in the winter.

JADE SEAL OF THE SHUNZHI
EMPEROR (R. 1643–1661) OF
THE QING DYNASTY WITH BOXES

Height 11.6 cm (4.5 in)
Length along edge 12.5 cm (4.8 in)

Inner box: height 33.6 cm (13.1 in)
Length along edge 28 cm (10.9 in)

Outer box: height 34.5 cm (13.4 in)
Length along edge 40 cm (15.6 in)

Shenyang Palace Museum

This was manufactured in the first year of the
kangxi era (1662). It was made to record the
honorific, temple, and posthumous names of the
Shunzhi emperor, then stored in the Imperial
Ancestral Temple. The inscription on the bottom
is in Manchu and Chinese.

**JADE TABLETS OF THE QING DYNASTY
EMPEROR SHIZU, THE SHUNZHI EMPEROR
WITH BOXES**

Length 28.6 cm (11.1 in)
Width 12.8 cm (5 in)
Thickness 0.9 cm (0.3 in)
Total thickness 11 cm (4.2 in)

Inner box: height 29.5 cm (11.5 in)
Length 36.5 cm (14.2 in)
Width 23.5 cm (9.1 in)

Outer box: height 36 cm (14 in)
Length 46 cm (17.9 in)
Width 31.5 cm (12.2 in)

Shenyang Palace Museum

This was made in the first year of the *kangxi* era (1662). It records the honorific, temple, and posthumous names of the Shunzhi emperor together with a biography. After manufacture, it was stored in the Imperial Ancestral Temple. The inscriptions are in Manchu and Chinese.

RECORD OF IMPERIAL GENEALOGY

Genealogy: length 89 cm (34.7 in)
Width 50 cm (19.5 in)
Thickness 23 cm (8.9 in)

Shenyang Palace Museum

This genealogy was compiled during the Qianlong
era and records the relationships of the imperial
family.

SET OF SIXTEEN BELLS WITH FRAME

Height of each bell 26.7 cm (10.4 in)

Shenyang Palace Museum

This set of bells was manufactured in the eighth
year of the Qianlong era (1743). It is an
instrument used for the performance of ritual
music during the Qing dynasty.

SET OF SIXTEEN JADE CHIMES WITH FRAME

Length of shorter section of each chime 23.5 cm (9 in)
Length of struck section of each chime 35.2 cm (13.7 in)
Width 1.9–4 cm (0.7–1.5 in)

Shenyang Palace Museum

This set of chimes was manufactured in the
fifty-fourth year of the *kangxi* era (1715) and was
used in the performance of ritual music during
the Qing dynasty.

SPECIAL JADE CHIME WITH FRAME

Height of chime 48.8 cm (19 in);
Width 89.7 cm (34.9 in); thickness 3.4 cm (1.3 in)

Shenyang Palace Museum

Manufactured in the twenty-sixth year of the Qianlong era (1761), this chime was used in the performance of ritual music during the Qing dynasty. There were twelve such chimes, each sounding one of the standard pitches, and only one was displayed during each month.

SET OF SIXTEEN OBJECTS OF THE HONOR GUARD

Shenyang Palace Museum

These objects were manufactured during the Qianlong era and used by the honor guard. They were displayed in the palace during important ceremonies and carried whenever the emperor traveled.

Pair of Round Fans in Imitation Song dynasty Brocade
Height 400 cm (156 in); width 100 cm (39 in)

Pair of Gold-Lacquer Ceremonial Axes
Height 274 cm (106.8 in)

Pair of Gold-Painted Lances
Height 400 cm (156 in)

Pair of Brocade and Satin Banners with Bronze Caps
Height 400 cm (156 in)

Pair of Flags with Green Fields
and Gray Borders Decorated with Satin
Height 400 cm (156 in)

Pair of Flags with Embroidered Gold Dragons
Among Clouds Decorated with Flowers
Height 400 cm (156 in)

Pair of Blue and Green Flags Decorated
with Dragons Among Clouds
Height 400 cm (156 in)

Pair of Brocade Banners
Height 400 cm (156 in)

Pair of Gold-Lacquer Spears in the Form
of Vertical Hands
Height 274 cm (106.8 in)

Pair of Gold-Lacquer Spears in the Form
of Horizontal Hands
Height 274 cm (106.8 in)

Pair of Blue Parasols with Nine Dragons
Height 400 cm (156 in)

Pair of Red Parasols with Nine Dragons
Height 400 cm (156 in)

Pair of Peacock Feather Fans
Height 400 cm (156 in)

Pair of White Swan Feather Fans
Height 400 cm (156 in)

Pair of Blue and Yellow Parasols Decorated
with Flowers of the Four Seasons
Height 400 cm (156 in)

Yellow Dragon Parasol with Curved Pole
Height 400 cm (156 in)

BRIGHT YELLOW SATIN IMPERIAL ROBE WITH MULTICOLORED EMBROIDERY AND EMBROIDERED SLEEVES

Length 137 cm (53.4 in)

Shenyang Palace Museum

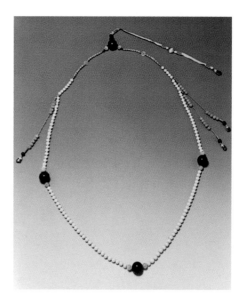

PEARL COURT NECKLACE

108 pearls
Length 80 cm (31.2 in)

Shenyang Palace Museum

This was manufactured during the Qianlong era and was worn by the emperor over ceremonial robes.

BLUE SATIN IMPERIAL ROBE WITH MULTICOLORED EMBROIDERY

Length 113 cm (44 in)

Shenyang Palace Museum

This is a ceremonial robe worn by the Qing emperor Dezong, who reigned during the *guangxu* era (1875–1908).

**APRICOT YELLOW *KESI* SILK
COURT ROBE FOR EMPRESS**

Length 137 cm (53.4 in)

This was manufactured during the Qianlong era and is a ceremonial robe worn by an empress in the palace on important occasions.

BRIGHT YELLOW SATIN
IMPERIAL DRAGON ROBE WITH
MULTICOLORED EMBROIDERY

Length 137 cm (53.4 in)

Shenyang Palace Museum

This is a ceremonial robe worn by the Qing emperor Renzong (r. 1796–1820), who reigned during the Jiaqing era.

PAIR OF LARGE STONE LIONS

Qing dynasty

Height 275 cm (107.2 in); frontal width 128 cm (49.9 in); length 171 cm (66.6 in)

Stone carving found in the Imperial Park in Beijing

China Cultural Relics Coordination Center

The lion is among the many auspicious animals in China. They were not native to China proper but were imported from India along with Buddhism during the Eastern Han dynasty (A.D. 25–220). The first lions were brought to China in the first year of the *zhanghe* era of the Eastern Han emperor Zhangdi (A.D. 87). From then on, lions were cast as symbolic guardians in Buddhism and placed as supporting figures at the base of Buddhist images. As the custom of lavish burials spread, emperors and aristocrats erected stone statues of people, horses, and elephants at their tombs to demonstrate dignity and rank. Beginning in the Western Han period, stone *bixie*—strange animals with wings and horns similar to tigers and leopards—were also placed at their tombs, and by the Tang period (A.D. 618–906), realistic statues

of horses and camels were placed there as well. From then on, lions became a prevalent feature of tomb architecture. During the Song, Liao, Jin, and Yuan dynasties (960–1368), lions also became an important element in palace architecture. During the Ming and Qing dynasties (1368–1911), both the placement of lions in palace architecture and their form became standardized. On the left was the male lion whose front right leg rests atop an embroidered ball. On the right was a lioness whose front left leg was placed atop a young lion. The two were posed looking inward, and were seated on bases resembling embroidered cushions. These lions were carved during the early Qing dynasty, and were probably placed on each side of a grand gate in the imperial park in the western suburbs of Beijing.

CEREMONIAL CARRIAGE

Qing dynasty

Length 400 cm (156 in)
Width 125 cm (48.7 in)
Height 211 cm (82.2 in)

Shenyang Palace Museum

Manufactured in the Qianlong era, this carriage was used to transport an image of the Buddha during ceremonies held in the imperial family temple in Shenyang during the Qing dynasty.

TWENTY BRICKS FROM THE GREAT WALL

Ming dynasty

Length of each 38 cm (14.8 in)
Width 19 cm (7.4 in)
Thickness 8 cm (3.1 in)

Excavated in Changping district, Beijing

China Cultural Relics Promotion Center

These bricks from the Great Wall are called "gray bricks." Three bear the inscription, "Manufactured in Shenzhou in the twelfth year of the Wanli emperor" [1584]. The Great Wall was formally begun during the Qin dynasty. It is immense in scale—one of the only man-made structures visible from the moon. As a result of the major construction efforts of the Qin, Han, and Ming dynasties, it reached a length of more than 3,100 miles, or more than 10,000 Chinese *li*, so it was called the "Great Wall of 10,000 *li*." The last great construction of the wall occurred during the Ming dynasty when construction also reached its highest technical level. From the first year of the Hungwu emperor (1368), when the founding ruler of the Ming, Zhu Yuanzhang, issued an order to repair the wall, construction continued for over two centuries until its completion during the reigns of the Jiajing and Wanli emperors. It extends more than 4,500 miles from the Yalu River, on the border between China and Korea, westward to the foot of the Qilian Mountains in the Hexi Corridor in Gansu province.

The northern border of China was never limited by the Great Wall. Rather, it was a line dividing the agricultural from the nomadic cultures and was intended as a defensive line for the central imperial dynasties against the incursions of various nomadic tribes.

Index

Suggested Reading

Birrell, Anne. *Chinese Mythology: An Introduction*. Baltimore: Johns Hopkins University Press, 1993.

Capon, Edmund. *Qin Shihuang: Terracotta Warriors and Horses*. Clayton, Victoria: Wilke and Company, Ltd., 1982.

Caroselli, Susan, ed. *The Quest for Eternity*. Los Angeles and San Francisco: Los Angeles County Museum of Art and Chronicle Books, 1987.

Chan, Albert. *The Glory and Fall of the Ming Dynasty*. Norman: University of Oklahoma Press, 1982.

Chang, Kwang-chi. *Art, Myth and Ritual: The Path to Political Authority in Ancient China*. Cambridge: Harvard University Press, 1980.

_____. *The Archaeology of Ancient China*. 4th rev. ed. New Haven: Yale University Press, 1986.

Clayre, Alasdair. *The Heart of the Dragon*. Boston: Houghton Mifflin, 1984.

Cotterell, Arthur. *The First Emperor of China*. London: Macmillan, 1981.

Deydier, Christian. *Chinese Bronzes*. Translated by Janet Seligman. New York: Rizzoli, 1980.

Elisseeff, Danielle, and Vadime Elisseeff. *New Discoveries in China: Encountering History Through Archeology*. Translated by Larry Lockwood. Secaucus, N.J.: Chartwell Books, 1983.

Fairbank, John King. *China: A New History*. Cambridge: Belnap Press of Harvard University Press, 1992.

Falkenhausen, Lothar von. *Suspended Music: Chime Bells in the Culture of Bronze Age China*. Berkeley: University of California Press, 1993.

Fong, Wen, ed. *The Great Bronze Age of China*. New York: Metropolitan Museum of Art and Alfred A. Knopf, 1980.

Gascoigne, Bamber. *The Dynasties and Treasures of China*. New York: Viking Press, 1973.

Gernet, Jacques. *A History of Chinese Civilization*. Translated by J. R. Foster. New York: Cambridge University Press, 1982.

Han, Zhongmin, and Hubert Delahaye. *A Journey Through Ancient China*. London: Muller, Blond and White, 1985.

Hsu, Cho-yun, and Katheryn M. Linduff. *Journey into China*. Washington, D.C.: National Geographic Society, 1987.

Huang, Ray. *China: A Macro History*. Rev. with epilogue. New York: M. E. Sharp Inc., 1990.

_____. *1587, A Year of No Significance: The Ming Dynasty in Decline*. New Haven: Yale University Press, 1981.

Kahn, Harold L. *Monarchy in the Emperor's Eyes: Image and Reality in the Ch'ien-lung Reign*. Cambridge: Harvard University Press, 1971.

Keightley, David N., ed. *The Origins of Chinese Civilization*. Berkeley: University of California Press, 1983.

Kerr, Rose, ed. *Chinese Art and Design*. London: Victoria and Albert Museum, 1991.

Kessler, Adam Theodore. *Empires Beyond the Great Wall: The Heritage of Genghis Khan*. Translated by Bettine Birge. Los Angeles: Natural History Museum of Los Angeles County, 1993.

Kuwayama, George, ed. *Ancient Mortuary Traditions of China*. Los Angeles: Los Angeles County Museum of Art and University of Hawaii Press, 1991.

_____. *The Great Bronze Age of China: A Symposium*. Los Angeles: Los Angeles County Museum of Art, 1983.

Li, Xueqin. *Eastern Zhou and Qin Civilizations.* Translated by K. C. Chang. New Haven: Yale University Press, 1985.

Lim, Lucy, ed. *Stories from China's Past: Han Dynasty Pictorial Tomb Reliefs and Archaeological Objects from the Sichuan Province, People's Republic of China.* San Francisco: The Chinese Culture Center of San Francisco, 1987.

Little, Stephen. *Realm of the Immortals: Daoism in the Arts of China.* Cleveland: Cleveland Museum of Art and Indiana University Press, 1988.

Liu, Laurence G. *Chinese Architecture.* New York: Rizzoli, 1989.

Loewe, Michael A. N. *Chinese Ideas of Life and Death: Faith and Reason in the Han Period.* London: George Allen and Unwin Ltd., 1982.

Los Angeles County Museum of Art. *The Quest for Eternity: Chinese Ceramics from the People's Republic of China.* Los Angeles: Los Angeles County Museum of Art, 1987.

Ma, Chengyuan. *Ancient Chinese Bronzes.* Edited by Hsio-yen Shih. Hong Kong, Oxford, and New York: Oxford University Press, 1986.

Merson, John. *The Genius That Was China.* Woodstock, N.Y.: The Overlook Press, 1990.

Nott, Stanley C. *Chinese Jade Throughout the Ages.* Tokyo: Charles Tuttle, 1977.

Paludan, Ann. *The Ming Tombs.* New York: Oxford University Press, 1991.

Pirazzoli-t'Serstevens, Michele. *The Han Dynasty.* New York: Rizzoli, 1982.

Powers, Martin J. *Art and Political Expression in Early China.* New Haven: Yale University Press, 1991.

Qian, Hao, Heyi Chen, and Suichu Ru. *Out of China's Earth: Archeological Discoveries in the People's Republic of China.* Edited by Patricia Egan. New York: Harry N. Abrams, 1981.

Rawson, Jessica. *Ancient China: Art and Archaeology.* London: British Museum Publications, 1980.

Schloss, Ezekiel. *Ancient Chinese Ceramic Sculpture: From Han Through T'ang.* 2 vols. Stamford: Castle Publishing Co., 1977.

Strassberg, Richard E. *Inscribed Landscapes: Travel Writing From Imperial China.* Berkeley: University of California Press, 1994.

Sullivan, Michael. *The Arts of China.* 3rd ed. Los Angeles: University of California Press, 1984.

Thorp, Robert L. *Son of Heaven: Imperial Arts of China.* Seattle: Son of Heaven Press, 1988.

Vitello, Gregory, ed. *Archaeology in China.* South Melbourne: Macmillan, 1977.

Waldron, Arthur. *The Great Wall of China: From History to Myth.* Cambridge and New York: Cambridge University Press, 1992.

Watts, James C. Y. *The Arts of Ancient China.* New York: Metropolitan Museum of Art, 1990.

_____.*Chinese Jades from Han to Ch'ing.* New York: Asia Society, 1980.

Weng, Wan-go, and Boda Yang. *The Palace Museum Peking: Treasures of the Forbidden City.* New York: Harry N. Abrams, 1982.

Whitfield, Roderick, ed. *The Problem of Meaning in Early Chinese Ritual Bronzes.* London: University of London, 1993.

Yu, Zhuoyun, ed. *Palaces of the Forbidden City.* New York: Viking Press, 1982.